ATLAS *of*
Rare Birds

ATLAS *of*
Rare Birds

DOMINIC COUZENS

The MIT Press
Cambridge, Massachusetts

First published in North America by The MIT Press. Published in the
United Kingdom by New Holland Publishers (UK) Ltd.

MIT Press books may be purchased at special quantity discounts for
business or sales promotional use. For information, please e-mail
special_sales@mitpress.mit.edu or write to Special Sales Department,
The MIT Press, 55 Hayward Street, Cambridge, MA 02142.

The materials presented in this book and the geographical
designations employed are not necessarily the views of
BirdLife International or The MIT Press.

Library of Congress Cataloging-in-Publication Data

Couzens, Dominic.
Atlas of rare birds / Dominic Couzens.
   p.   cm.
Includes bibliographical references and index.
ISBN 978-0-262-01517-2 (hardcover : alk. paper)
1. Rare birds. 2. Rare birds—Geographical distribution. I. Title.
QL676.7.C68   2010
598.168—dc22
                                        2010017197

Reproduction by PDQ in the UK
Printed and bound in Singapore by Tien Wah Press

Front cover: Houbara Bustard.

Back cover: Regent Honeyeater.

Page 1: Spoon-billed Sandpiper.

Page 3: Ultramarine Lorikeet.

Opposite: Tristan Albatross.

Page 6: (from top) California Condor, Kagu, Montserrat Oriole,
Whooping Crane and Regent Honeyeater.

Page 7: (from top) Spoon-billed Sandpiper, Gurney's Pitta, Udzungwa
Forest Partridge, Bruijn's Brush-turkey and White-eyed River Martin.

CONTENTS

INTRODUCTION

Opposite: Gurney's Pitta.

Left: Seychelle's Magpie-robin.

This book tells the stories of 50 of the rarest birds in the world. By its very nature, it is a book of its time, and there is every chance that several of its characters could not be included in a future edition a few years along the line. Some of the featured birds are teetering on the brink of extinction, and several may be extinct already. In the 10 chapters you can read the stories of how they came to become so rare, and how they are faring now.

So what makes a bird rare? Well, to regurgitate and remix the words of the great English playwright William Shakespeare: some are born rare, some achieve rarity, but most have rarity thrust upon them. The ones born rare are those naturally found in just a single small corner of the planet, such as an island or a particular lake or marsh. The second group have struggled to cope with their natural world; many have entered this category – and indeed have become extinct – by the natural ebb and flow of their fortunes as they compete for space against other birds, or fall to predators, or are wiped out by disease or disaster. However, most of the world's current rarest birds, and most of those featured in this book, have found their way into the endangered category simply by falling foul of us – people. Humanity's drives are frequently detrimental to the environment, as we all know so well, and a given bird's rarity is merely a single measure of this.

So, in its way, this book is also about the clash between birds and people, past and present. This has always been an uneasy relationship. While birds are universally admired and appreciated by people all around the world, equally nowhere are they entirely safe. The stories in this book imply that there is not a single place, from the deepest corners of the continents to the most isolated of islands, where birds don't seem to suffer at our hands, even if it is only indirectly. If you were to observe the situation from outer space, you might conclude that people aren't good for birds. We hunt them, shoot them, cause them to become sick, drive them out of their habitat, and now, just for good measure, we are mucking up their climate.

Yet of course, this isn't the complete picture. One of the great achievements of the 20th century – a century notable for its terrible inter-human violence on an unprecedented scale – was the rise of the conservation movement, in its many forms. Beginning modestly, environmentalism has leapt up humanity's agency in the most extraordinary way, so that now it is part of the talk of world leaders, something that no-one in power can politically ignore. As conservation has become important, so it has become more powerful, more resourced and richer. By the middle of the 20th century there were already those who were prepared to offer money and time for the benefit of iconic species such as the California Condor and the Kakapo, and at the same time create large networks of nature reserves. Now a whole raft of species are being kept alive in the conservation incubator, their individual fortunes cared about and followed by thousands of interested people.

This book tells some of their stories. Others, meanwhile, have kept so clear of humanity that their fortunes are barely known. Part of this book concerns the species that have kept the lowest profile of all, those that have evaded discovery until only recently, or have kept out of our way so effectively that we had decided that they must be extinct. The accounts of how these birds have surfaced or resurfaced to science are fascinating, and often decidedly strange. Who, for example, would have expected scientists to discover a new species at the bottom of a camp cooking-pot?

While conservation is, if nothing else, one of the great human success stories of recent times, other stories in this book remind us not to be complacent. The world is changing frighteningly fast, not only in ways that have historically compromised bird populations – habitat destruction, pollution, hunting, the introduction of non-native predators or competitors – but now with the inexorable march of climatic amelioration, in ways that are new and difficult to understand. While we must always keep an eye on species that appear vulnerable, such as migrants and those found on islands, we must be careful to watch all birds with concern. There is now, and there increasingly will be, a tendency for currently common birds to plummet in population, and we must

Left: A rare colour image of a male Ivory-billed Woodpecker, taken by James T Tanner in the USA in the 1930s.

be ready for such catastrophes. Rarity and vulnerability are not necessarily the same thing.

One of the great weapons against impending extinction in birds is the knowledge about what is happening and the fostering of concern about all species. To that end, the book is dedicated to the many individuals and agencies who bring conservation to people's awareness and take action in the field. Special tribute should be paid to Birdlife International and its many partners around the world. Much of the empirical information in this book is taken from its website: www.birdife.org, while details of its work can be found on pages 12-13.

My hope in writing this book is that, in its small way, it will also contribute to conservation. If just a few people are prompted by reading this to take more action or contribute more money to the preservation of birds, then it will have done its job.

DOMINIC COUZENS, DORSET, UK. AUGUST 2010

BirdLife International

Birdlife is the world's largest global alliance of bird conservation organisations that share the same mission: to conserve wild birds, their habitats and global biodiversity. As a worldwide community, we work together across a wide range of conservation actions – working with governments on global issues like climate change, or local actions such as protecting specific species and their habitats.

With around 2.5 million members and 8 million supporters worldwide, our network of more than 100 national organisations together are the leading authority on the status of birds, their habitats and the issues and threats facing them.

The BirdLife Network is pulling together to build a brighter future for the world's 10,000 species of birds, all of whose lives and futures are inextricably linked with people. With one in eight of the world's birds threatened with global extinction, many species need a helping hand to prevent them from going extinct.

PREVENTING EXTINCTIONS

The BirdLife Preventing Extinctions Programme is spearheading greater conservation action, awareness and funding support for all of the world's most threatened birds, starting with the 192 species classified as Critically Endangered, i.e. those in the highest threat category. Central to the programme is the development of two new communities; BirdLife Species Guardians, composed by experts who will take the lead in conserving threatened species in their own countries, and BirdLife Species Champions, made up by organisations or individuals who will raise awareness for and fund the vital conservation that is so urgently required.

HOW YOU CAN HELP BIRDLIFE

There are many ways in which you can help fund our work and every donation, however large or small, makes a difference.

BirdLife urgently needs your donations now towards our Species Champions initiative if we are to save the 192 Critically Endangered species identified as being most at risk of global extinction. Many of these birds are predicted to become extinct within the next 10 years. Help us to stop this.

BirdLife and its Partners know what actions need to be taken. What we need are the necessary funds to make the conservation happen.

Below: Launched in 2006, BirdLife's Albatross Task Force has already made great inroads into bridging the gap between fisheries and conservationists in stopping albatross and other seabird species bycatch.

Right: After an absence of more that 200 years, the Rimatra Lorikeet was returned to the Pacific island of Atiu in 2007, in a shining example of conservation and co-operation. The Queen of Atiu was an enthusiastic participant in the project.

- £15 can pay for a 100 seedlings for a reforestation project in Africa to improve the natural habitat for rare birds
- £200 can buy 1 hectare of forest to protect at least one pair of globally threatened birds in Asia such as the Fairy Pitta (*Pitta nympha*)
- £650 can pay for vital field equipment to help conservationists in the Middle East
- £1,250+ can pay for costs of a habitat survey in South America and a rare bird reintroduction programme

Please support our work by donating.

If you are a resident of the USA please make checks payable to 'American Friends of BirdLife International Inc' and post to American Friends of BirdLife Inc, c/o Chapel & York, PMB #293, 601 Pennsylvania Ave. NW, Ste 900, South Bldg., Washington DC 20004, USA.

American Friends is an independent charitable organisation with separate 501 (c) 3 status which enables US residents to receive direct tax benefits for contributions made to support the work of BirdLife International in the Americas and globally.

UK residents, please make cheques payable to BirdLife International and post to: BirdLife International, Wellbrook Court, Girton Road, Cambridge CB3 0NA, UK.

Alternatively you can donate securely on line by visiting *www.birdlife.org* and click the link 'How to help'.

For more information please email *howtohelp@birdlife.org* or telephone *+44 (0) 1223 277318.*

1 BACK FROM THE BRINK

Starting again with just a few survivors

Seychelles Magpie-robin

How far can a species sink before recovery is impossible? If the stories here are anything to go by, the answer would seem to be very low indeed. Every one of the five birds covered in this section has had, at one time or another, a world population of 80 individuals or less. In every case they have recovered to something a great deal healthier, and in every case this has been achieved by intensive management by conservationists.

This section should be a tribute to the efforts of those both at the sharp end and the blunt end of conservation: the scientists, captive breeding specialists, the publicists and those who have provided funds. Although the stories might all sound dramatic when told in a few words, the truth behind the headlines is a great deal of hard slog by a lot of dedicated people. For example, what about the business operative who gives the money but never actually sees the results? Such people are heroes.

There is, though, a danger in being too cheered by these stories of coming back from the brink. The brink is not a good place to be, and not every story like this will have a happy ending. A low population is not normal, or desirable. The aim should always be to be proactive, and prevent conservation efforts from becoming crisis management.

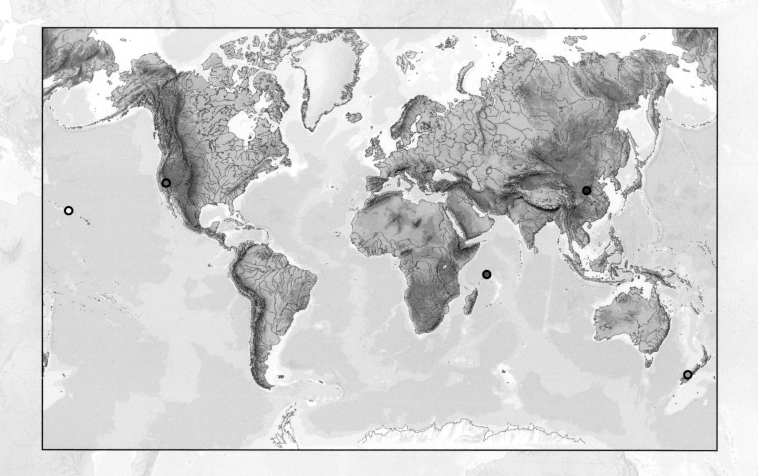

CALIFORNIA CONDOR
Gymnogyps californianus

The survival of the relic

If you should look up into the skies above California, Arizona or Mexico these days and spot the formidable, broad-winged silhouette of a California Condor, you can be certain that you are watching a link with North America's most ancient past. That's because the California Condor, one of the world's largest land birds, has been part of this south-western landscape for well over two million years. While Ice Ages came and went on the North American continent, floods and earthquakes shaped the land and vast herds of animals arose and perished below, in all that time the California Condor rose above the upheaval, and survived. It has lived all the way from the barely imaginable past until now. Few extant bird species have such a long history.

However, it is fair to say that the California Condor's past is also its glory. In the late Pleistocene it ruled the skies, together with a host of other related New World vulture species, some of which were the largest birds ever to take wing – a extinct vulture from Argentina, for example, had a wingspan of between six and eight metres. These monster scavengers fed off the ample carcasses of the late Pleistocene megafauna. The grasslands supported herds of mammoths, horses and camels, which were predated upon by sabre-toothed cats and outsized wolves, while in the open woodlands giant sloths quietly grazed. When such animals died their bodies provided, at a stroke, large chunks of meat, enough to support an unrivalled assemblage of scavenging birds.

From about 10,000 years ago, however, the climate cooled and precipitated the extinction of this biomass bonanza. Most of the dependent vulture species died out completely, but the California Condor did not. Its range contracted sharply, but it held on. Where once it had occurred right across the continent east to Florida and New York, now it retreated to the mountainous west, from British Columbia to Baja California. In place of mammoth meat, it relied on the carcasses of mountain lions, sheep and, on the coast, beached whales and sealions. It was a relic of its

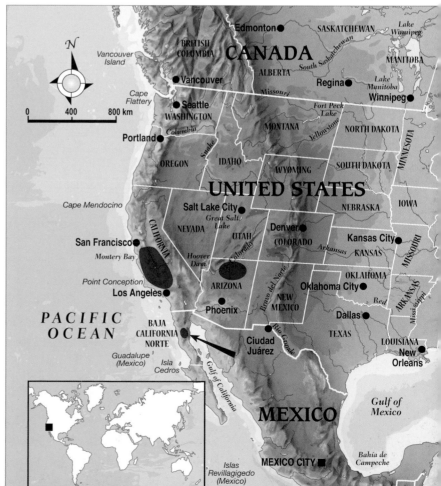

Opposite: The bare head and neck of the California Condor is typical for a scavenger. Any feathers on the head would soon get soiled and damaged by the blood and entrails of the corpses it devours.

Left: California Condor is one of North America's largest birds, with a wing-span of more than 2.7m; the dark head indicates that this bird is a juvenile.

imperious past, but at least it was a living one.

However, its fortunes nosedived once again with the arrival of European settlers to western North America. There were all sorts of reasons for this. In those less enlightened times any large bird with a hooked bill was perceived as a threat to people's precious livestock, so the condor was shot at and trapped, and its nests were destroyed. At the same time, with so many people moving on to the land, there was less room and less prey available for condors, and their core habitat – open woodland, plains and uplands – was diminished and degraded. You might say that the condor didn't fit the rapidly developing modern world. Any species that cannot breed until it is at least six years old, and even then does not necessarily lay its single egg every year, will instantly be in trouble when at odds with an unsympathetic human populace. High mortality and low recruitment to the population is a recipe for rapid extinction. By the early 1900s, a decline in the population of the great birds had already been noted.

What looked like the final countdown for this ancient species came into sharp relief with efficient

CALIFORNIA CONDOR
Gymnogyps californianus

monitoring of its numbers in the 1950s, when only 150 individuals were known to be in existence. By 1968 this figure was down to 60 and by 1978 to 30, barely a viable population. It looked as though two million years of occupation was about to come to an unceremonious end.

However, the conservation movement had fully awoken by this time, and the California Condor's status as one of the rarest birds in the world bestowed on it a certain type of glamour to add to its undeniable charisma as a very large, supreme flying bird. At the eleventh hour a California Condor Recovery Team was formed (in 1973), and by 1980 a very intensive and well-funded programme began the painstaking process of bringing the California Condor back from the brink of extinction. The effort was just in time; there were 22 birds left in the wild, plus a couple in captivity. Any longer and the subsequent story would have been very different.

Nowadays, when many people around the world have already heard about the successful turnaround for California Condors to the present, it is easy to forget how risky the Recovery Plan was at the time, and how much the condor's fortunes repeatedly hung by a thread. Most readers will have heard that the birds were saved by captive breeding at the San Diego Wild Animal Park and at Los Angeles Zoo (and subsequently at the Peregrine Fund facility at Boise, Idaho, and at Oregon Zoo). Yet no California Condor chick had ever hatched in captivity before the first in 1988, well after the programme had been instigated. Furthermore this breeding breakthrough occurred the year after the last wild condor had already been captured. The total commitment to captive breeding

was a bold and brave move, and there was never any guarantee that it would work.

Nevertheless, as the world watched, the California Condor population began to grow in captivity. The zookeepers developed specialized techniques to improve success. They removed eggs from the condor nests as soon as these had been laid, encouraging the females to lay a replacement egg and double their reproductive output, while the first egg was kept in an incubator. Finding out that condors did best when raised by their parents, the keepers developed special puppets mimicking condor heads to use whenever they fed the chicks, and played tapes of adult condor calls as they did so. Once the techniques had been perfected, the breeding programmes were producing 25–30 young condors a year. Gradually the number of birds rose enough to raise the prospect of reintroducing some birds back into the wild.

Finally, in 1992, after a five-year hiatus, California Condors once again flew in the wild in their namesake state, in Los Padres National Forest near Monterey, this time with a substantial pool of captive birds in place behind them. Many of the original threats to the wild predecessors remained, most especially the threat of poisoning from lead shot in carcasses. But despite this, the reintroduced population has been built up significantly. At the time of writing there are 189 birds in the wild in four main sites, including Arizona's Grand Canyon area and in Baja California, Mexico. There are also still 169 birds in the breeding programmes.

Two main recent developments give particular hope for the future. First, in 2002, the reintroduced birds bred in the wild for the first time, and there are

Above: The California Condor's broad wings with distinctive 'fingers' enable it to soar and glide for great distances in search of food.

Left: Some of the last remaining wild California Condors survived on the coast, where they fed on beached carcasses. Fittingly, some of the first reintroduced birds were released around Los Padres National Forest along the spectacular Big Sur.

now breeding attempts every year (although, at the moment, with little to show in terms of surviving chicks). Second, in July 2008, the state of California prohibited the use of lead shot in the areas where the condors occur. If this policy can be introduced throughout the United States (it will, inevitably, be vehemently opposed by the powerful National Rifle Association, because alternatives, such as copper or tungsten bullets, are more expensive), then the future of the condors will be much more rosy.

However, in context, the California Condor is still in a sorry state, and remains Critically Endangered. Ironically, it now relies on the care and ingenuity of one of those species whose remains, along with the mammoths and sabre-toothed cat carcasses, it would no doubt have once eaten frequently. Then it was king of the skies. Now it is just about hanging on.

KAKAPO
Strigops habroptilus

Booming at last

The Kakapo has been teetering on the very edge of extinction for longer than almost any other known species of bird. A huge, goose-sized parrot confined to New Zealand, its plight was recognized as long ago as 1896, when the remarkable pioneering conservationist Richard Henry translocated 300 of these giant psittacids onto Resolution Island, offshore from Fiordland, in the south of South Island; even then he already worried that the once numerous and widespread mainland population was being decimated by a suite of introduced predators such as rats, stoats and dogs. This prescient project failed when Stoats (*Mustela erminea*) made it to the island in about 1900. During all the long years between then and now, this particular bird has become almost synonymous with the struggle against extinction.

The Kakapo has become an icon of conservation, and that identity is entirely appropriate. And yet the riveting story of its survival should not cloud another aspect of the Kakapo that is easily overlooked: its quite amazing natural history. Here's just one fact to grab you from the start: the Kakapo is probably the longest-lived bird in the world. Recent studies suggest that the average life-expectancy is 90 years, and that many Kakapos live for a great deal longer than that – longer than albatrosses, vultures and anything else. At the same time, this parrot also has the lowest metabolic rate of any bird known. It is, if you like, the giant tortoise of the bird world.

Evolving in a land without any mammalian predators at all, the Kakapo is large, slow-moving and flightless. For much of its life all it has to do is to leave its roost-site and walk to some suitable greenery upon which it can graze, since it is completely vegetarian. It

Opposite: The owl-like face of the Kakapo betrays its status as one of only two parrots in the world that are completely nocturnal.

Above: The area around Mitre Peak in New Zealand's spectacular Fiordland was one of the Kakapo's last natural refuges.

will often chew at leaves, rhizomes and stems on the ground, but it is an excellent climber and frequently feeds in shrubs and low trees, clambering about using its strong claws and balancing by flapping its otherwise useless wings. It is quite at home above ground and has been recorded 30m up in the canopy of forests – not bad for a bird that cannot get airborne.

The Kakapo presumably once had to deal with some avian enemies because it does not walk around conspicuously or brazenly. Far from it – it is an extremely elusive creature. It is cryptically coloured in barred shades of green, and its feeding forays are secret and completely silent and made under cover of darkness. Being one of only two parrot species in the world that are completely nocturnal, the Kakapo is one of a minority of bird species that has an acute sense of smell. This helps it to detect the best and most nutritious vegetation available at the time.

If you are slow, cryptic and nocturnal, breeding can

KAKAPO
Strigops habroptilus

potentially be a problem, simply because of the difficulty of coming across a mate. Male Kakapos solve this problem in an extraordinary way: they make a sound, a low booming, that can carry for up to 5km and thus be broadcast to a reasonable number of listening females. In order to ensure good transmission of the sound, each male selects a site on a ridge overlooking a valley, and excavates a series of bowls about 60cm in diameter, each linked by tracks that the bird maintains itself. When booming from these bowls, the males ensure that their signals are amplified. Good transmission sites are always in short supply, and the males bicker over them, sometimes indulging in quite serious fights. However, the territorial males are still closely clustered, allowing the female to make a choice as to her favourite singer. She visits her chosen bird at the cluster of boomers (the 'lek') and mates with him only; henceforward she is responsible for all the other breeding duties alone.

The actual breeding of the Kakapo is something of an event. It doesn't take place every year – far from it; when a bird lives to 90 years nothing needs to be done in a hurry. Only when a very good food supply can be guaranteed throughout the six- to eight-month nesting cycle will be birds be tempted to reproduce, something that in natural conditions happens only once every six years or so. This usually follows a previous summer of good rains, so that the Kakapo's favoured foods, such as Rimu (*Dacrydium cupressinum*) will produce a heavy fruit and seed crop. Then the females will site their nest in a burrow under a tree root and lay a couple of eggs.

Unfortunately, a slow breeding rate, coupled with natural fussiness and a ponderous, flightless lifestyle, has made the Kakapo extremely vulnerable to any kind of ecological change. In contrast to many of New Zealand's rarities, its problems began long before European settlers arrived. It was the Maoris, arriving on the islands a thousand years ago and bringing dogs and Pacific Rats (*Rattus exulans*) with them, that started the trouble. The Maoris were efficient hunters and they also cleared and burned extensive areas of scrub. Thus, by the time settlers came from Europe in the late 18th century, New Zealand's countryside was already under siege, and the Kakapo was already rare. Black Rats (*Rattus rattus*), stoats and cats added to the army of predators, and introduced herbivores chewed up the indigenous forests. Before the end of the 19th century the Kakapo, along with a good many other New Zealand natives, was already in serious trouble.

Remarkably, the Kakapo's plight very quickly captured people's imagination and some very early attempts were made to translocate the birds to predator-free islands. Although Richard Henry's was the first attempt, it was followed by several others. Three birds were introduced to Little Barrier Island, off North Island, as long ago as 1903; three more were released onto Kapiti Island in 1912 and survived for 24 years. There was then a long gap until 1974, when two released on Maud Island formed the beginnings of a reintroduction attempt there (eventually to include five birds).

However, despite these valiant efforts, the translocated Kakapos never succeeded in breeding on their new territory. At the same time, the mainland population was on its last legs, restricted now to Fiordland, the remote mountainous underbelly of South Island. A thorough count, using helicopters to

Above: Although flightless, the Kakapo uses its wings for balance when climbing trees and bushes. The current population of more than 120 birds is protected on carefully managed offshore islands.

ship biologists in, was made in 1976, and came to the gloomy conclusion that there were only 18 Kakapos remaining in the wild and, tragically, that they were all males.

Of course, this would have signalled the certain end of the Kakapo except for a sensational event the following year. Amazingly, an unknown Kakapo population had been thriving all along, on the ornithologically well-known Stewart Island, off the south coast of South Island. It was estimated that about 150 birds remained – an incredible boost to the bird's survival. And not only this, but there were at least 20 females among them, the first Kakapos of this gender to have been seen for at least 70 years.

The Stewart Island birds were discovered just in time. Their population was soon revealed to be diminishing rapidly, mainly because of the depredations of feral cats, and there was very little breeding taking place. In 1982 the New Zealand Wildlife Service decided to move every single one of the surviving birds to cat- and stoat-free offshore islands, such as Codfish Island (off Stewart Island) and eventually Maud Island. But although the survival rate of the eventual 60 evacuees was high, rats prevented much breeding success, and those birds that did breed did not produce enough young to offset any natural losses from the population.

In 1995, after the population had sunk to a low of 51 birds, a Kakapo Recovery Plan was launched and extra funding for captive breeding and care of wild-living birds was secured. Considerable money and scientific work has been ploughed into the efforts of the National Kakapo Team, and this has at last yielded some results. After several excellent breeding seasons (especially 2002), the total population of Kakapos currently lies at 124 birds. And for the first time in at least 100 years, the survival of the species is now likely for the foreseeable future.

LAYSAN DUCK

Anas laysanensis

The narrowest squeak of all?

If pure numbers are the best measurement of being on the brink of extinction, then the Laysan Duck probably holds the record for the narrowest squeak from oblivion of all. In the year 1930, if records are to be believed, the species was down to just one surviving female (with several males) – and that,

surely, is just about as perilous as you can get. That the species managed to escape from such a fix is nothing short of miraculous.

However, it did so. In the year in question the lone female managed to do what the species needed it to do, and laid a clutch of eggs. However, disaster soon struck when the eggs were found by a migratory Bristle-thighed Curlew (*Numenius tahitiensis*), and eaten – bad luck indeed, for the nests of Laysan Ducks are usually exceptionally well hidden in thick vegetation and hard to find. At this point it would have been reasonable to suppose that the species now depended on the survival of this single female for a whole extra year before the new breeding season, with all the danger of predation, disease or mishap that that implied. But the fit female surprisingly managed to lay another clutch of eggs a few weeks later, and this time the chicks made it beyond the juvenile stage. From these small beginnings the species turned a corner.

Over the next few years the population crept up, inbreeding notwithstanding. The minute atoll of Laysan, the ducks' only home, was no longer occupied by guano-mining workers and was now uninhabited, and protected as a bird reserve. By the 1950s there were enough birds on the island for some to be taken into captivity, and the descendants of these founders are still present in a few collections today. By the beginning of the 1990s there were more

Left: The fortunes of the Laysan Duck once depended upon the last remaining female. In this pair the male (behind) can be distinguished because it has brighter orange legs and more prominent head markings than the female.

than 800 individuals on Laysan and the species was apparently thriving – in relative terms, at least.

But then, in 1993, disaster struck again, as a double-whammy this time. The island was overcome by a drought which drastically reduced the food available to the birds – they subsist, oddly, mainly on brine-flies, moths, beetles and shrimps, and feed on just one saline lagoon in the middle of the island, mainly at night. At the same time, botulism broke out among the adult birds, causing high mortality. Once again the species fell back to critical levels of population, with possibly as few as 82 birds remaining – better than in the 1930s, but still dangerously low.

The problem for the Laysan Duck had never, it seemed, really gone away. With just one population on a single small, very isolated atoll of just 370ha

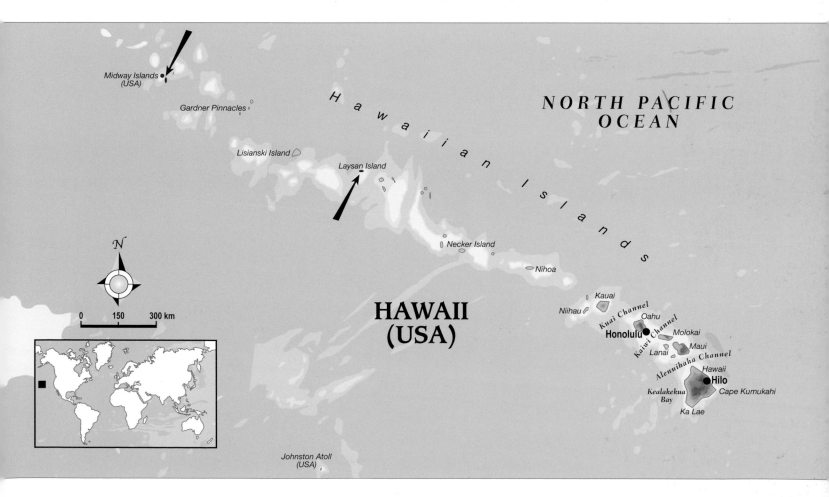

LAYSAN DUCK
Anas laysanensis

(3km long) and in the middle of the Pacific Ocean (the nearest island is 500km away), the Laysan Duck would always be a sitting duck, potentially to be killed off even by a localized disaster. Disease among the population, the introduction of a mammalian ground-predator or a major weather or oceanographic event could all wipe the species out in a single strike. In such a backwater, with nowhere to go, the Laysan Duck seemed destined always to fluctuate between the plain and the precipice.

However, it wasn't always this way. Recent subfossil finds have shown that the species was once widespread throughout the Hawaiian archipelago. While in recorded history the bird has only ever been found away from Laysan on the equally isolated Lisianski Island, almost 1,700 km to the west of Honolulu, and then not since 1834 (the record is not universally accepted), the conclusion is that it must

Right: In the wild, the Laysan Duck nests in dense vegetation and only the female tends the chicks. On Laysan Island there is only one small lake, which is where the entire population lives. The ducks feed mainly upon the dense population of brine flies.

Opposite: Midway island has proved to be a true paradise for a translocated population of Laysan Ducks.

have been wiped out from the other islands before it was formally recorded. But this discovery showed that the Laysan Duck is not the one-island endemic that it was previously thought to be, and perhaps not such an ecologically fussy species either.

Thus, in 2004, conservationists intervened. A programme began to settle the Laysan Duck onto Midway, another protected atoll even further out into the Pacific. As an initial experiment, 42 individuals were released there and the first results have been spectacularly encouraging. The ducks have thrived, partly because they are less crowded than on Laysan, and they started breeding immediately: more than 50 chicks were fledged in the very first season.

With a little human help, the future of the Laysan Duck suddenly looks a good deal brighter. Having established the species on Midway, plans are afoot to establish a translocated population on Lisianski, although as yet there is not enough wetland habitat

for a viable population to live there. And from this point, who knows? Perhaps there are other places, even on the main Hawaiian Islands, where the Laysan Duck could be reintroduced in the future? It may well be that, within a generation, conservationists will have little to worry about for this attractive and resilient species – a far cry indeed from the desperate situation of the 1930s.

In an ironic twist to the story, the species that almost administered the *coup de grace* to the Laysan Duck is now thought to be in a certain amount of trouble itself. The Bristle-thighed Curlew only breeds in south-western coastal Alaska, and makes an extraordinary transoceanic migration to the islands of the Central and South Pacific. Numbers in 2000 were estimated at about 10,000 birds and declining; it would be extraordinary indeed if, one day, the numbers of Laysan Duck were to exceed those of the curlew on its way down.

SEYCHELLES MAGPIE-ROBIN

Copsychus sechellarum

Safety through island-hopping

To have one species on a small archipelago on the verge of extinction is perhaps understandable, given the many problems that birds often face on islands – small range, low population, introduced vegetation and introduced predators, for example. But to have four birds that need to come back from the brink over the years could almost be construed as careless – not that it was the fault of the birds, or of the conservation agencies that tried to protect them. But that is exactly what has happened on the Indian Ocean island group of the Seychelles. First an owl,

then the magpie-robin, then a warbler and then a white-eye have flown to the precipice of extinction and so far, every one has come back again. The efforts of conservations in this part of the world deserves to be recognized worldwide.

Each case has been intriguing, and each case is different. The first endemic bird of this group of 40 granite islands to be declared doomed was the Seychelles Scops Owl (*Otus insularis*). It had been discovered in 1880 and seen only once in the ensuing 78 years before, in 1958, it was officially designated

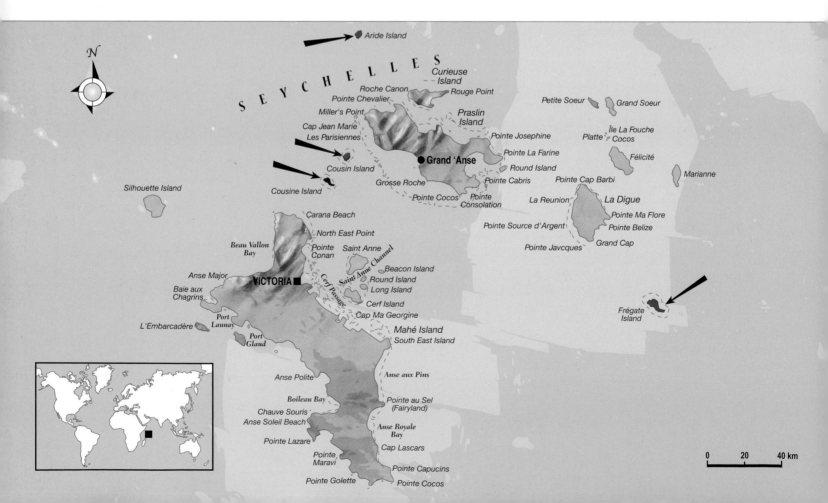

extinct. Then, slightly embarrassingly, it was rediscovered only a year later, with a world population estimated at 20 birds on the main island of Mahé. Actually, this proved to be a serious underestimate and, with the steady regrowth of suitable habitat, following a decline in the cinnamon, coconut and logging industries, there are now thought to be about 300 birds.

The case of the Seychelles Warbler (*Acrocephalus*

Above: Once reduced to a population of 12-15 birds, the Seychelles Magpie-robin has recently been reclassified from 'Critically Endangered' to 'Endangered' by BirdLife International.

sechellensis) was always much more desperate. Once widespread on several islands, a combination of destruction of scrub and forest, together with the depredations of Black Rats (*Rattus rattus*) eradicated this sensitive bird from every island except one, the

●●●●●●●●●● ●●● **SEYCHELLES MAGPIE-ROBIN**
Copsychus sechellarum

minute 0.3km² Cousin Island, in the centre of the archipelago. In 1968 its population had slumped to just 30 individuals in a swamp on the edge of the island. But then Cousin came up for sale and, after a huge campaign by conservationists, was purchased by the then International Council for Bird Preservation (now BirdLife International). Ever since then the island has been transformed from a coconut plantation into a supremely well-managed bird reserve, with its habitat transformed and predators kept at bay, and the warbler population has leapt to over 300 birds, with others being translocated to other islands.

The Seychelles White-eye (*Zosterops modestus*) was written off at least twice, between 1935 and 1960, when it was assumed extinct, and then more recently in the late 1990s, when the population on Mahé, the only known outpost, had fallen to 35 birds. Since Mahé is a relatively large 30km-long island, the causes of its decline, forest destruction and then a twin threat from predatory Black Rats and competition for food from the aggressive, introduced Common Myna (*Acridotheres tristis*), were not containable in a way they could have been on a smaller island, and the future looked very grim indeed. Then, extraordinarily, a large (more than 250 birds) and overlooked population was discovered on Conception Island in 1997. This island was predator-free, and from this pool of birds the white-eye has been carefully nurtured and introduced onto other islands.

However, perhaps the most fraught story of all the Seychelles sagas, and the one that undoubtedly caused conservationists more fear and stress at the time than any other, was the case of the Seychelles Magpie-robin. This particular species was a little more fussy than some, occurring preferentially in coastal closed-canopy woodland with not much understorey but a rich, insect-laden leaf-litter. It occurred on at least seven islands to begin with, but the usual catalogue of deforestation and introduced predators, particularly cats and rats, triggered its almost complete disappearance. By 1965 the only birds left were on the isolated eastern island of Frégate (2.19km²), and there were only 12–15 of them in all. Furthermore, there were cats present on the island, licking their lips; the mainly ground-foraging magpie-robin was extremely vulnerable to them.

The conservation agencies had to sweat torturously hard and long for the magpie-robin's continued existence. Apart from keeping cats at bay, not a great deal happened for a number of years, despite efforts to translocate some individuals to other islands, and the population remained in the danger zone. However, the birds were resilient and, helped by their unusually long lifespan for such a small bird, up to 10 or more years, the population did not succumb to extinction. In 1982 cats were finally eradicated from Frégate, but the magpie-robins didn't benefit because by now the habitat had degraded into thick scrub and was not ideal for the birds. In fact it wasn't until 1990, with the population still only 23 individuals, that a proper recovery programme was implemented, organized by BirdLife International and Britain's Royal Society for the Protection of Birds. This plan concentrated on clearing non-native scrub and planting native forest trees, and it paid quick dividends; by 1994 there were 48 birds. The success spawned renewed attempts to translocate some

Left: The Seychelles Magpie-robin occurs in mature forest with a thick canopy and a well developed layer of leaf-litter.

Below: With 40 granite islands and over 100 coral or sand islets, the isolated Seychelles islands host a wide range of endemic animals and plants. This is Cousine.

magpie-robins to other islands, first to Aride, where it failed at first, and then to Cousin and its neighbour Cousine, where small populations were established. Meanwhile, a rat eradication programme continued on Frégate and the population carried on climbing. There are now over 180 birds in existence, on the four islands, including Aride.

The sheer effort required in turning around the Seychelles Magpie-robin's fortunes should never be underestimated. For a start, it has been an impressive collaboration between the conservation agencies both local and national, as well as the islands' owners and the Seychelles government. The number of man-hours has been astronomical, in such activites as habitat management and restoration, eradicating pests, designing predator-free nest-boxes, giving the magpie-robins supplementary feeding, as well as all the logistics of transferring birds between islands. And, in 2005, all the hard work by people and magpie-robins together resulted in the species being downlisted from Critically Endangered to Endangered, a very symbolic achievement. Truly, the Seychelles Magpie-robin is back from the brink.

CRESTED IBIS
Nipponia nippon

Nippon tuck

There can be few more diverting sights in the ornithological world than a pair of Crested Ibises in full breeding regalia, busying themselves on their treetop nests overlooking a rural wetland in north-east China. Yet only a few years ago the world had more or less given up on ever seeing this delightful scene again. The Crested Ibis was down to the last few individuals, and hope was fading for the survival of the species.

As with so many species of perilously threatened birds, the Crested Ibis has suffered from a long, slow decline from a starting position of relative comfort. At the beginning of the 20th century it was a reasonably common over a range embracing Japan, north-east China, the Koreas and extreme south-east Siberia. Some of these populations were sedentary, others migrated to southern parts of China for the winter. Their main requirements have never been particularly exacting; all they needed was a few large trees or woodland well within reach of wetlands or rice-fields rich in small aquatic creatures, such as fish, amphibians, freshwater crustaceans and insects. Their favourite trees for nesting were pines.

However, several forces began working against them from the turn of the last century onwards, some specific to them and others that affected millions of other birds just as much. The specific problem was hunting for the plumage trade. Ibises are pretty spectacular birds to look at, and the Crested Ibis is one of the most interesting of all, with its fine white plumes on the back of the head. Ibises are quite slow-moving birds, probing their bills into the mud with an air of detached indifference, and then flying with slow wing-beats at a measured, somewhat regal pace. As such they must have been easy targets for hunters desperate for an income from bird plumes.

At the same time, in the early years of the 20th century, that part of Asia where the Crested Ibis occurs began to experience an explosion of the human population. Inevitably, this put pressure on all habitats, not least those where the ibis occurred. Pine forests, the ibis's favourite nesting sites, were devastated and marshes were drained. As the century

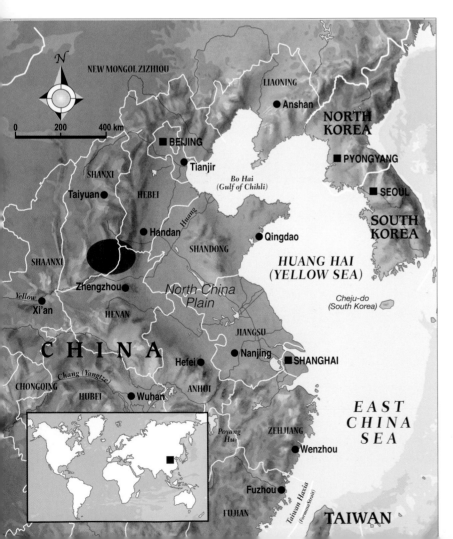

Left: Perhaps the most famous of all of Asia's rarities, the Crested Ibis has teetered on the brink of extinction for decades.

wore on, the region also underwent the convulsions of political change, some of which, such as the Chinese Great Leap Forward of the 1950s, had negative repercussions for birds (it led to a famine). Over in Japan, in 1934 the Japanese government decreed that the ibis, the country's national bird and a species that had been revered by the Shoguns of the 19th century, would be protected – although unfortunately the decree did not extend to its forest habitat. But in the Second World War and its aftermath, few gave much thought for the welfare of birds. In Japan, there was a massive use of pesticides and agrochemicals to try to sustain the ravaged human population. As the human world suffered, so the Crested Ibis began tumbling towards a dangerously low population level.

When the world emerged from the worst of the

turbulence, the wreckage wrought upon the ibis could finally be assessed. The Siberian population had evidently long gone, probably since the early days of the century. In Japan in 1953, a mere 31 birds were counted. In China there were still a few around in 1958, but a couple of years later there were none seen at all, and it was considered to be extinct in the country. It seemed that the formerly large breeding range, encompassing many thousands of birds, had contracted to one small part of Honshu where there were now only a handful. If the Crested Ibis was going to survive, its renaissance was up to the Japanese.

Things did not begin well. Although fully protected in Japanese law, the ibises that were in the wild weren't thriving, and the population continued to nose-dive, down to only 10 wild birds by 1961. The

CRESTED IBIS
Nipponia nippon

Crested Ibis was now officially the rarest bird in the world. In this desperate situation, the government finally set up a nature reserve for the birds, on Sado Island, where most of the last birds lived. At the same time, a captive breeding programme was begun, comprising the single bird now left on the mainland and three Sado birds. It was a complete failure. All but one of the birds died within a few weeks, apparently from being fed an inappropriate diet, and the situation began to look bleak. The years dragged on without any more captures, with the onus on the wild birds to reproduce. They didn't. Instead, some died from pesticide poisoning. By 1981 there were only five birds left. Forlornly, these birds were all captured in case, by some miracle, they could be persuaded to breed. But in truth, the days of this species were quickly ticking down. It was only a matter of time before these relatively long-lived birds eventually died off one by one.

That would have been the end of the sorry saga had it not been for the persistence of the Chinese Academy of Sciences, who decided to mount a search for any remaining ibises that might, against the odds, still be lurking in their country. It took three years, and an estimated 50,000km of travel before, in a quiet corner of Shaanxi Province, the scientists struck gold.

Opposite: The ibises use their long, curved bills to probe in marshy areas for fish, frogs, molluscs and insects. Productive wetlands with neighbouring tall trees for breeding are all they need to survive.

Below: Every nesting tree of the Crested Ibis is state property in China and the birds are protected in the breeding season by guards.

They found two breeding pairs of the Crested Ibis on a quiet hillside, and these had three young between them. With commendable speed, the Forestry Ministry took over and formed an Ibis Protection Station near the breeding pairs. Soon a smattering of other pairs was found and, perhaps even more importantly, the authorities introduced regulations to prevent logging, ban the use of firearms locally and prohibit the use of agrochemicals where the ibises were found to feed. By 1987 every nesting tree – and by now there were 51 in total – was declared as state property and therefore fully protected. These days the nesting trees are guarded during the breeding season, just to make sure that the birds are safe.

From this germ of rediscovery, a full-blown recovery has been born and the fortunes of the Crested Ibis have reversed in quite spectacular style. The former 'rarest bird in the world' is still Endangered, but no longer Critically Endangered. Not only are the birds beginning to do better in the wild, but under the stewardship of Beijing Zoo they are now being bred successfully in captivity. The most recent estimate has been of about 500 birds in the wild, and about 150 individuals in captivity. There has even been some co-operation between the Chinese and Japanese, despite their famously frosty relations, with the Chinese sending birds to Japan to augment the latter's captive breeding population.

What the story of the Crested Ibis tells us is that, with a great deal of effort and political will, most species of birds can probably be saved. But perhaps it also helps if a few pairs of any species hide themselves away in a quiet treetop, away from the attention of the world.

2 THE PERILS OF ISLAND LIVING

Many threatened birds are confined to small spaces.

Junin Grebe

Islands, with their restricted space and isolation, have proven a double-edged sword for birds. While lying in oceans of solitude allows islands to become pressure cookers for speciation, it also makes them unusually vulnerable to disturbance of all kinds. The end result is a large number of endangered species: indeed, about a quarter of all the threatened birds in the world are found on islands.

And what birds they are! Some of the most remarkable species that have ever lived have been confined to islands. On islands evolution proceeds more or less unchecked and, it seems, makes outlandish forms as if drunk on its own creative juices. Think of the astonishing avian treasures that occur today on Madagascar or Papua New Guinea, on the West Indies and on the islands of Oceania.

But think too of the island species that have been lost. There are a disproportionate number of them. Think of the Dodo (*Raphus cucullatus*) and its relative the Rodrigues Solitaire (*Pezophaps solitaria*) from the Mascarene Islands; the astonishing Elephant Bird (*Aepyornis maximus*) of Madagascar, perhaps the largest bird that ever lived; and think of the whole family of Moas (Dinornithidae), found only in New Zealand, a group of tall flightless birds that arose in the predator-free idyll of New Zealand. All of them became extinct shortly after people invaded their refuges. Even today, exactly where these birds' feet trod, other species continue to struggle for survival.

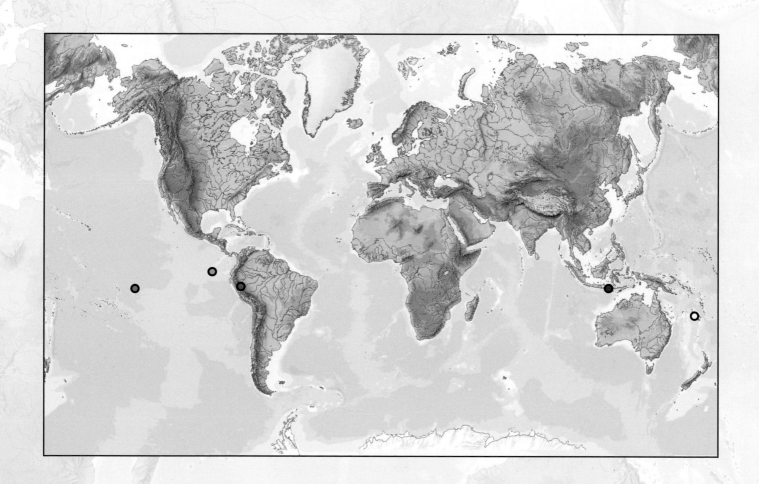

ULTRAMARINE LORIKEET
Vini ultramarina

At risk in Polynesia

Few birds in the entire world can match the implausible colour scheme and pattern of the glorious Ultramarine Lorikeet. Whether in the wild, in a cage or in a book, the mixture of turquoise, blue and white, set off by the orange bill and feet, never looks quite real. It's the sort of improbable bird you might dream up in your imagination.

If you did dream it up, the chances are you would do so as an inhabitant of some far-off land, perhaps a tropical island in the South Pacific. And that, it so happens, is exactly where it does live. It is only found in the Marquesas Islands, an almost impossibly remote archipelago of 12 volcanic islands and islets that lie further from continental land than any other island group in the world. They are in the middle of the Pacific Ocean about 1,000km north of the Equator, a mind-boggling 4,850km from the coast of North America, and even further away from Australia or Asia. They are 1,200km north-east of Tahiti, which is itself a truly remote part of the earth's surface; both sets of islands are politically part of French Polynesia.

Only a handful of the world's ornithologists have ever set eyes on a wild Ultramarine Lorikeet. This is hardly surprising, since the mere act of getting to the Marquesas Islands is a feat in itself, and for most, a very expensive one at that. In truth, the lorikeet is just one of a suite of Pacific island birds that remain, even today, extremely poorly known and appreciated. Yet many are extraordinarily beautiful and spectacular, and some are edging perilously close to extinction.

One might think that isolation could be a buffer against the ills of the world but, sadly, this is far from the case. It is suspected that the Marquesas were already inhabited by the time of Christ, probably from Tahiti, well before they were 'discovered' by the Spanish in 1595. Long-term human settlement has wrought its usual destruction on the lowland forests, not just from clearing for settlement but, more pervasively, by the grazing of livestock, especially goats. These days there isn't much natural vegetation left intact.

Happily for the Ultramarine Lorikeet, the destruction is not totally complete. There is still some

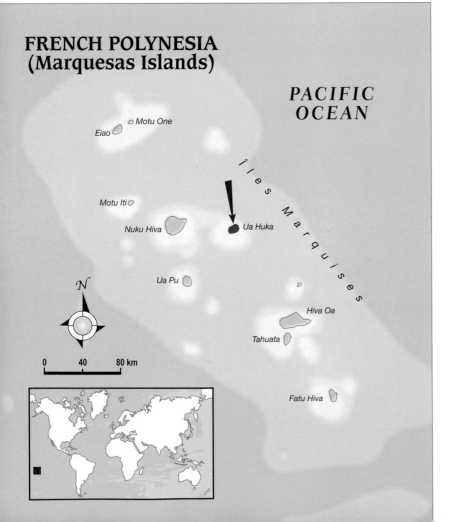

FRENCH POLYNESIA (Marquesas Islands)

PACIFIC OCEAN

Motu One
Eiao
Îles Marquises
Motu Iti
Nuku Hiva
Ua Huka
Ua Pu
Hiva Oa
Tahuata
Fatu Hiva

N

0   40   80 km

highland forest left and, besides, this small parrot can also cope with some artificial habitats, such as coconut plantations. In common with other parrots, it is primarily vegetarian and will take fruit, buds and flowers.

You might expect, therefore, that the Ultramarine Lorikeet is well equipped to cope with the modification of its isolated island home. But there is a serious problem, one that is instead pushing this

Above: The stunning Ultramarine Lorikeet exemplifies everybody's idea of an improbably coloured tropical bird.

stunning bird towards the abyss of extinction. Along with the colonization of people came a still more pernicious threat, the Black Rat (*Rattus rattus*). This mammal, a native of tropical Asia, is more arboreal than the other introduced rat species that occur on Polynesian islands, and it has a special penchant for

ULTRAMARINE LORIKEET
Vini ultramarina

Right and opposite: In common with other members of its family, the Ultramarine Lorikeet is vegetarian, feeding on fruit, buds and flowers.

Below: The isolation and beauty of Polynesian islands often masks a history of disturbance and degradation of habitat.

eating the eggs and young of nesting birds. The lorikeets, which nest in holes in trees and sometimes in hanging coconut shells, suffer badly from their depredations.

The sheer effect of rats on the Ultramarine Lorikeet has been graphically shown on two of the Marquesan islands. On Ua Pou, a small island in the central group, for example, there was an estimated population of 500–600 Ultramarine Lorikeets in 1975. However, Black Rats were accidentally introduced in 1980, and the species was not found at all on Ua Pou in a survey in 1998; it thus took the predators less than eighteen years to eliminate the population. On another island, Fatu Hiva, the southernmost of the chain, 29 Ultramarine Lorikeets were introduced between 1992 and 1994 in the hope of creating a viable population on a sparsely inhabited island. The experiment started well, with 51 individuals counted in 1997. But the presence of rats on Fatu Hiva was confirmed for the first time in 2000, and only seven years later this population, too, was extinct.

The same story can be re-told for the main island, Nuku Hiva. Although it is not known when rats arrived here, the Ultramarine Lorikeet population was estimated at 70 birds in 1975. There are none today.

The truth is that there would be no wild Ultramarine Lorikeets left in the world today at all had it not been for the actions of a Marquesan teacher in the 1940s. He decided to introduce a single pair of lorikeets to the island of Ua Huka, where, for unknown reasons, there had been none present previously. The birds flourished in the rat-free environment and, happily, they flourish still. From the two parents the birds went forth and multiplied, Adam and Eve style. The most recent survey, in 2004, estimated between 1,763 and 2,987 individuals.

But these birds are absolutely on a knife-edge. Their one remaining refuge is an island with an area of only 78km². It is quite mountainous (up to 857m) and inhabited by some 570 people. There are regular boats from the main island and, ominously, there are rats on a small island just a few hundred metres offshore from Ua Huka. It would not be dramatising the situation too much to claim that these couple of hundred metres are what stands between the Ultramarine Lorikeet and extinction. These, plus a professional rat-catcher and a few rat traps.

The case of the Ultramarine Lorikeet is not unique. Polynesia, in essence, is a world of incredibly isolated islands, each with its own signature birds and plants found nowhere else in the world. All of them are frighteningly vulnerable, often to small and accidental events such as the introduction of rats. It so happens that many Polynesian endemics are singularly beautiful. The Ultramarine Lorikeet is probably the most eye-catching of all, but there is a fine array of unique pigeons, other parrots and rails, too. In many ways, it is an oceanic wonderland, ripe for intensive study and curative conservation action. But equally, the fauna could be seen as a set of jewels, about to be cast carelessly into oblivion.

FLOREANA MOCKINGBIRD

Nesomimus trifasciatus

Under siege in the Galapagos

There can hardly be any more famous archipelagos in the world than the Galapagos Islands. It was here, 800km off Ecuador, that the celebrated English scientist Charles Darwin landed in 1835 from the ship the HMS *Beagle*, his mind ripe with youthful enquiry. It was partly his observations on the local fauna that fuelled his seminal book *On the Origin of Species*, published in 1859. The book, of course, elucidated for the first time the theory of evolution by natural selection, and in doing so changed the way that we all see ourselves.

Any student of biology, and especially evolution, will have heard of Darwin's finches, the small, dark-brown passerines that inhabit the islands and have bills neatly matched to suit their differing lifestyles. Indeed, the very fact that they are called Darwin's finches suggests that these were the dominant animal group that led Darwin to his famous theory. But in fact this is not the full story at all. Darwin didn't pay the finches much attention at the time of his visit, and it was only after his return to England that the importance of the finch specimens that he had acquired was recognized by the ornithologists of the time, notably John Gould. The birds weren't even called Darwin's finches until almost 100 years later, in 1936.

In fact, when Darwin was on his voyage it was the mockingbirds that caught his attention, not the finches. Recognising that they were similar but different from those he had seen on the South American mainland, he resolved to make careful note of where each island specimen came from. Reviewing them afterwards on board ship, he was astonished to find that all his specimens from Chatham Island (now San Cristobal) looked the same as each other, as indeed did those from Albemarle (Isabela) and Charles (Floreana) Island, but that the birds differed from island to island. There were evidently three species involved. It was this observation, together with similar variation in the local Giant Tortoises, that first triggered Darwin to wonder whether species were unchangeable (the dominant concept at the time), or whether they could, in fact, be modified. One can imagine how this germ of an idea eventually led to the theory of evolution. There is thus a strong argument to suggest that the mockingbirds contributed more to Darwin's thinking than the more famous finches.

Today North American visitors would doubtless recognize the size and shape of the Galapagos mockingbirds, but these island forms are otherwise very different to the familiar songbird. They are browner in colour, not grey, and they have streakier plumage with longer, down-curved bills. They also, perhaps surprisingly, lack the famous ability of the Northern Mockingbird (*Mimus polyglottos*) to imitate the songs of other birds.

That isn't to say, however, that they are duller and less interesting than Northern Mockingbirds. Far from it. Being island forms, they have expanded their niche and modified their behaviour in some curious and quite bizarre ways. While the Northern Mockingbird is omnivorous to the point of consuming both arthropods and fruit, the Galapagos Mockingbirds have expanded this tendency to less conventional extras. They frequently eat carrion, including young turtles, lizards, seabirds and their eggs, and even dead sealions. They scavenge for scraps among seabird

The breeding biology of the Galapagos mockingbirds is also intriguing. Rather than living as single pairs and defending an exclusive territory, as most small birds do, these mockingbirds live in long-lasting expanded groups, of different sizes according to species, which defend a collective territory. In three of the four species the dominant pair are aided at the nest by other members of the group, many (but not necessarily all) of which are previous offspring of

Above: The slightly sinister-looking Floreana Mockingbird has some extremely unusual feeding habits.

colonies. They are predators of seabird nestlings and small lizards. They collect ticks from the backs of marine iguanas and, in rather sinister fashion, the Española Mockingbird (*Nesomimus macdonaldi*) will drink the blood from wounds of boobies, sealions and iguanas. This species has also been observed trying to drink blood from leg cuts in human beings.

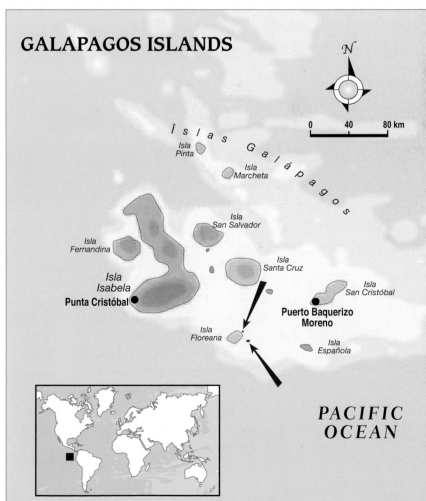

FLOREANA MOCKINGBIRD
Nesomimus trifasciatus

Right: Although there is only one bird in this picture, other Floreana Mockingbirds won't be far away. All individuals live in permanent social groups.

Opposite: The climate of the islands where the Floreana Mockingbird occurs is steadily becoming drier, and this is thought to be a contributing factor to the depletion the bird's population.

the pair. The usual arrangement is that only the dominant female lays any eggs in a given breeding attempt, although sometimes other females contribute. Once the chicks hatch, the rest of the group will help to feed the young, which have an enhanced chance of survival as a result. The most enthusiastic helpers are the dominant pair's offspring, and males tend to make the most effort. Females, once grown up, soon move on from the group and join a neighbouring one to maintain the genetic flow of the species.

Not surprisingly, given that most of these

mockingbirds live on small to medium-sized islands, their populations are rather limited in global terms. And while the birds on the islands of Isabela and San Cristobal are doing fine at present, those on the smaller refuges of Española and Floreana are much more vulnerable. Both are of serious conservation concern.

Unfortunately, the situation with the Floreana Mockingbird has now become critical. When Darwin found this species in 1835 it was still common on Floreana itself, but by 1888 it had disappeared completely. Although the cause isn't known for

certain, it is suspected that introduced Black Rats destroyed the population. Interestingly, the other islands with mockingbirds have native rats as part of their fauna, and they don't seem to have suffered in the same way. The wave of rat predation would have rendered the species extinct had it not been for the existence of mockingbirds on two satellite islands, Gardner-by-Floreana and Champion, and these are where it survives today.

It is only just holding on, though. The islands are only tiny, just 0.1km² in the case of Champion and 0.8km² in the case of Gardner, and naturally don't support many birds. Furthermore, the population has been declining because of recent El Niño climatic fluctuations that have rendered the islets drier and reduced the adult population, and this decline seems to be continuing. At the same time, avian pox has affected the population on Champion recently. By 2008 there were fewer than 50 birds left in the world.

Every bird extinction is a tragedy, of course. But the potential loss of the Floreana Mockingbird would have an additional poignancy. Having helped to set Charles Darwin's mind working, its place in the realm of science is secure; but its future is far less so.

KAGU

Rhynochetos jubatus

The living Dodo

There is something appealing in the notion of strange birds found only on remote islands. It seems appropriate, somehow, that in an isolated piece of land cut off from the rest of the world, curious and unique forms should arise in the splendour of their uncluttered domain.

Few birds in all the world fit so perfectly into this picture as the splendid Kagu of New Caledonia. It is quite unique – indeed, nobody seems entirely certain what it is and what it is related to. The most promising leads link it to the Sunbittern (*Eurypyga helias*), a colourful waterside bird of lowland South America, another species, incidentally, making up its own family of one. But there are few external similarities between the two birds, and you'd never guess any kind of relationship by looking at them.

Indeed, if you delve into the anatomy of the Kagu, where unexpected links between birds often show up, its uniqueness actually becomes even more magnified, not diminished. Strangely, for example, the Kagu seems to have unique blood, with a third the number of red blood cells, and yet three times the haemoglobin content of normal birds. Another oddity, this time shared with a few other families, is the presence of powder-downs. These are feathers that effectively disintegrate as they grow, acquiring the consistency of powder; they may help in waterproofing the plumage by absorbing the rain when it falls, as it frequently does in the tropical climate of New Caledonia. And for those who appreciate obscure trivia, the Kagu also has a unique nose. Or at least, it has flaps of skin over its nasal openings that are unlike those of any other bird in the world. These almost certainly keep them protected when the Kagu is probing into the soil.

Yet quite apart from this internal oddness, the Kagu just looks magnificently strange. It is tempting to think that, even if it didn't already exist, some work of fictional imagination might have dreamed it up anyway. About the size of a duck, it wanders around the forest floor on its long red legs in a slightly mechanical fashion, frequently stopping to look around or probe with its long and equally startlingly red bill. Its ashy-grey plumage looks surreal and out of

NEW CALEDONIA

Récifs d'Entrecasteaux

Récif Petrie

Île Suprise

Grand Passage

Île de sable

Île Pott

Île Art

VANUATU

Ouvéa

Îles Loyauté (France)

Île Lifou

SOUTH PACIFIC OCEAN

Nouvelle Calédonie

Maré

Noumea

Îles des Pins

Grand Récif du Sud

N

0   60   120 Km

Above: The threat display involves raising the crest and spreading the wings, the latter to show off the Kagu's grey-and-white striped primary feathers.

Left: The odd-looking Kagu is unique, with no close relatives.

place in the heavy litter of the forest floor, where most ground-feeding birds are camouflaged and skulking. The plumage is silky in texture and at times almost seems to shine. The staring eyes are bright red, and comparatively large; they are set well forward so that their fields overlap, conferring on the Kagu the ability to judge distance accurately in front of it, which helps it stab at the creatures of the forest floor. And finally there is that wild and wispy crest. At times it rests on the Kagu's back looking like a shawl, but when the bird is excited it is raised and makes its owner look like some heraldic griffin, somewhere between beautiful and ridiculous.

The wings of the Kagu are quite large but curiously not strong enough to support flight; the best a Kagu can manage is to glide downhill when trying to escape danger. However, that isn't to say that the wings aren't

used. They play a useful role when the bird is displaying or threatened, when they can be opened or waved about to reveal an expectedly rich pattern of dark grey and white bars. This pattern, together with the crest, makes the Kagu look even more spectacular.

Any student of conservation reading about a flightless bird on an isolated tropical island would almost automatically these days feel their heart sinking. However, the Kagu is alive and well and, although it is Endangered, it is not yet on the verge of extinction. New Caledonia is a large island and the Kagu has a historically wide distribution on it, and has so far managed to survive the ravages that have come with human settlement. Apart from deforestation, the Kagu has probably suffered most from interference from introduced mammals, particularly direct predation from dogs, which live on the outskirts of

KAGU
Rhynochetos jubatus

villages but wander widely. It is also thought that cats and rats may have a serious impact on young Kagus in the nest. Another major threat concerns alteration of habitat: one of the best localities for the Kagu is being seriously damaged by the grazing of introduced Rusa Deer (*Cervus timoriensis*).

However, the most famous site for Kagu, Rivière Bleue in the east of the island, still has a strong population. Dogs are controlled here and the numbers of Kagus are slowly increasing, with 500 recorded in 2007. What with about the same number dotted about the other main parts of its range, and some areas that might hold Kagus unaccounted for, the total

population of this unique bird undoubtedly exceeds the 1,000 mark. Not much, but for such a potentially vulnerable species, it bodes well for the immediate future at least.

There are echoes in the Kagu of another famous island species. The bizarre appearance, forest habitat, unique provenance, flightlessness, pale plumage: all these are shared with what is perhaps the world's most famous extinct bird, the Dodo (*Raphus cucullatus*). That species, from the island of Mauritius in the Indian Ocean, disappeared before 1650 and has been the subject of intense interest, excitement and speculation ever since. Yet currently in New

Left: The Riviere Bleu reserve is probably the best place to observe New Caledonia's most famous bird.

Caledonia lives a bird every bit as unique and bizarre, and perhaps more so. Had the Kagu become extinct as quickly as its Mauritian counterpart, no doubt it would be subject to the same posthumous intrigue.

You could almost say, though, that the Dodo is alive and well and living on an island off north-eastern Australia. This time, let's hope it stays around for a good deal longer.

Opposite: This bird, with its long crest raised, is performing its strutting threat display to a reflection of itself. The proximity of the human shows how confiding the birds can be.

Above: The Kagu feeds by standing over the leaf-litter, waiting for invertebrates to show themselves. Once it has spotted something, the bird will often run towards it and strike. The raised foot is sometimes used to disturb food by brushing the foliage.

JUNIN GREBE
Podiceps taczanowskii

Marooned on a watery island

The Junin Grebe is found only on a single lake in central Peru, the lake from which it derives its English name. You might wonder, therefore, why it is included in this section about island endemics. Well, from a conservation point of view there is no difference between an island and a lake: one is land surrounded by water, and the other is water surrounded by land. The effect is the same: isolation.

Right: Although Junin Grebes are flightless, they are powerful swimmers, attaining a top speed of 2m/s. This bird is stretching its leg and revealing the lobed toes that are typical of all grebes.

Below: In this stunning portrait, the plumes around the ear-coverts of this Junin Grebe indicate that it is in breeding plumage.

This grebe, occurring on just one water body in the whole world, is as vulnerable as any island species.

And interestingly, in the same way that many island forms, isolated from predators, have lost the power of flight over time – birds such as dodos (Raphidae) and kiwis (Apterygidae) spring to mind – so the Junin Grebe is also flightless. It cannot leave its only home on earth.

It is quite a location to call your headquarters. Lake Junin lies in the Peruvian Andes at a height of 4,088m, in the high-altitude puna zone, characterized by open, windswept tussocky grassland. It can be exceptionally cold here, but, to add to the overall harshness, it is also dry, especially in the Austral winter. Lake Junin is a shallow lake 143km² in extent, and bordered by enormous reedbeds, where the grebes build their nests.

Junin Grebes feed mainly on small shoaling fish (*Orestias* sp.), which become scarce when the reedbeds dry out. In order to catch them several grebes often work in unison, swimming forward in a line and diving synchronously so that the fish are confused and easier to catch. This co-operative hunting is a striking aspect of their behaviour. The birds mainly work in the open water of the lake close to mats of submerged vegetation, known scientifically as *Chara*, which provide optimum fish habitat. The hunters can swim extremely fast, up to 2m per second. On occasion, however, they will be less energetic and feed on easier-to-catch food items such as insects and their larvae, possibly doing this more in the off-season.

The birds usually breed between November and March, although this does depend on the prevailing conditions, and in some years there is no reproduction at all. As mentioned above, the nests are built on the outer edges of the lake's huge reed-swamp system, often where tall stems of rushes bend over and interlock to form completely impenetrable islands that are safe refuges. It seems that Junin Grebes are long-lived birds that do not attempt to reproduce quickly. A pair will only produce one clutch a year at most, laying a couple of eggs. In any

JUNIN GREBE
Podiceps taczanowskii

given year only about a third of all adults engage in any breeding at all.

Low recruitment to the population should not be a problem in long-lived birds if they are undisturbed and their environment is stable over a long period. However, unfortunately this is far from the case for Lake Junin, which suffers from two major disturbances caused by mining in the area. First, effluent from the mines causes pollution. Zinc levels affect the growth of *Chara* clumps, the water in the lake is gradually being contaminated by iron oxide sedimentation, and the bordering meadows have been affected by increasing copper levels. Already the northern end of the lake is uninhabitable, and in recent years fishermen have reported finding dead grebes floating in other parts, too.

The second problem is that water levels are managed by a nearby hydroelectric plant, which feeds energy to the mines. This arrangement is skewed towards the mines and rarely works in favour of the lake's ecosystem, especially when water is drawn away in dry years. In such conditions the reedbeds dry out and fish stocks fall, making it much harder for the Junin Grebes to find food. The birds do revert to feeding on invertebrates, but breeding is usually curtailed. The problem is exacerbated by fluctuations in climate caused by El Niño events, which often lead to long periods of very little rain, putting dual pressure on the lake's wildlife, which also includes an endemic rail (*Laterallus tuerosi*), giant toad (*Batrachophrynus macrostomus*) and catfish (*Pygidium oroyae*).

As far as the grebe is concerned, the real worry is the long-term pollution of Lake Junin, leading to the overall decline of the species (from at least 1,000 birds in 1961 to about 300 today), coupled with water-level drops. If, for example, there is a series of bad years without much breeding, the total population could fall to levels from which it might be extremely difficult for the grebe to recover.

As yet there is still hope for the Junin Grebe. On the whole, the local community is extremely keen for the Lake Junin ecosystem to be managed in a more sustainable way – after all, for many, their lifestyle depends on it. Lake Junin is recognized as a national reserve, with controlled hunting and fishing. The Peruvian government put forward emergency laws in 2002 designed to sustain the lake and, especially, curb water extraction, but this has had little or no effect so far. There has been international pressure. The Lake is a Ramsar site of global conservation importance, and several agencies, including BirdLife International and the American Bird Conservancy, continue to lobby the government. Efforts are also underway to urge tourists, especially birders, to visit the lake and its grebes.

At present the Junin Grebe is considered to be Critically Endangered, and there are plenty of reasons to be extremely concerned about its future. In the last few years three species of other range-restricted grebes have become extinct, the Colombian Grebe (*Podiceps andinus*) around 1977, the Atitlan Grebe (*Podilymbus gigas*) of Guatemala around 1990 and the Alaotra Grebe (*Tachybaptus rufolavatus*) of Madagascar around 1988, with many of them facing similar suites of difficulties as the Junin Grebe. The precedents are obvious. Birds that live on single lakes have a high extinction rate – just like island species, in fact.

Left: These grebes mainly hunt in open water adjacent to mats of submerged vegetation, searching for small fish.

Below: The waters of Lake Junin are under pressure from developments such as mines and hydroelectricity plants.

BALI MYNA

Leucopsar rothschildi

Too beautiful for its own good

As soon as a certain Erwin Stresemann, one of the greatest ornithologists of the 20th century, discovered the Bali Myna in 1911, there was no way that his bird could ever be ignored. It was simply too dazzling to look at, too unusual in its plumage. To say that it is pure white except for black on its wing and tail tips would be no more than understating bald facts: it is the intensity if the peppermint white that makes this bird seem to shine, and its copious crest and brilliant patch of blue skin around the eye just add to the Bali Myna's exotic demeanour. The species has always been admired by people, and this has been its problem ever since its discovery.

The very fact that the myna has only been known for a century is also a telling one when it comes to the tale of the bird's fortunes. It evaded previous discovery by only living on one small island, and even there not occurring widely. In 1911 it only occupied a 50km stretch along the north-west coast of Bali, and the highest wild population estimate ever made did

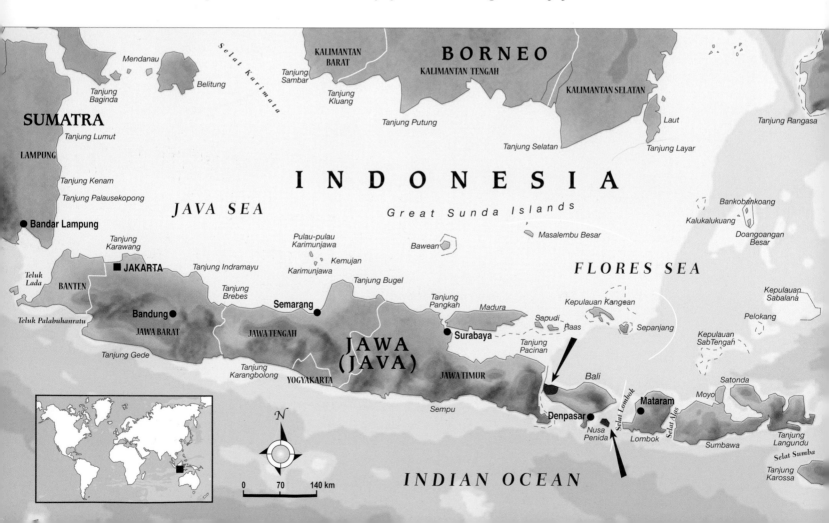

not exceed 900 birds. It seemed to prefer places away from people, and had probably always been a rare bird.

The trouble was that its rarity and beauty made a potent combination, especially for those who liked to keep birds in cages. The Bali Myna, as its name suggests, is a member of the starling and myna family (Sturnidae), a group that takes well to captivity and is entertaining for its antics and pleasing voices. Many species are easy to breed. So all in all, the Bali Myna is a very desirable species for bird collections: it is an aviculturist's dream.

Nobody quite knows when the Bali Myna's numbers began to tip towards Endangered levels, but by the 1970s the population did not exceed 200 individuals, all at one locality, Bali Barat on the north-west side, which covers about a tenth of the island.

Above: The Bali Myna has long been admired in the cage-bird trade for its good looks and pleasing voice.

The reasons for the decline are much easier to fathom, though. Aside from some forest destruction outside the park, the birds disappeared because they were repeatedly trapped for the cage-bird trade, where they commanded high prices. In 1970 it became illegal under Indonesian law to trap and trade the birds, but of course the demand made it tempting for people to continue taking birds from the wild.

Throughout the next few years the Bali Myna kept a foothold in Bali Barat, which became a national park in 1982 (although this did not improve the bird's fortunes). Here it occurred, and occurs still, in open woodland with a grassy understorey, and breeds in old woodpecker holes in trees. Pairs of mynas appear to

BALI MYNA

Leucopsar rothschildi

stay together throughout the year; they often sit side by side and preen each other in a show of companionship. They are territorial when breeding during the rainy season between January and March, and both sexes take part in building the nest and raising the young. With plenty of room in a large and quite well protected national park, the birds should

have been able to maintain a viable population.

But this simply didn't happen. By 1988 the population of Bali Barat had fallen to 47 individuals, by 1989 to 23 and the following year to 15. The Bali Myna was racing to extinction in the wild. Already a Bali Myna Project had been set up in 1983 to try to captive-breed the birds on-site, and releases from the

project raised the population to about 50 shortly afterwards. But nothing could stop the abuses, and in 2001 the wild population, despite regular releases, fell to only six individuals.

The Bali Myna Project seemed permanently to be afflicted by one crisis or another. In its earlier years it was repeatedly mismanaged and subject to corruption. Then, in 1999, the compound used to house the mynas prior to release into the wild was raided by an armed gang, who stole more than 30 birds. There was another attack in 2006 and the guard on duty bravely fought off the intruders and was injured. None of the birds was taken, but it did show up the risks guards were having to endure. With prices on the black market reaching US$2,000 per bird, the stakes were high.

The population in the national park is relatively buoyant at present, with perhaps 50 birds in the monsoon woodland. As the example above proves, the guarding of the birds is more effective these days, and the whole Bali Myna Project could be said to have proven a persistent defender of the birds. Plans to legalize the trading of captive Bali Mynas may well be put in place soon that will make it much less lucrative to poach birds from the wild. If the market is flooded (the birds are easy to breed), it is possible that incidents of trapping will reduce.

They are unlikely to cease altogether, though, and the best future for wild-living Bali Mynas might now lie elsewhere, in what has proven to be a somewhat unexpected success story. In 2006, 37 birds were released into a bird sanctuary on Nusa Penida, an island off the south-east coast of Bali that is most famous as a diving destination. The island is drier than its neighbour, and at first nobody was sure whether the birds would adapt to it. They have, however, proved both resilient and enterprising: they have surprised scientists by nesting in palm and fig trees instead of relying on cavities made by other birds.

But the real advantage of Nusa Penida is its human culture. When the first birds were released they were offered to the gods by Hindu priests in a formal religious ceremony. Local traditional laws promote respect for the wildlife, and the whole community is entrusted with protecting the birds. When the Bali Mynas were introduced, all 35 local villages signed bird protection laws, and the communities agreed to enforce fines on offenders and, on occasion, ostracise such people. There are now 100 Bali Mynas on Nusa Penida and it seems they are well protected.

After a hundred years of persecution, the Bali Myna, it seems, has finally found its refuge.

3 THREATS IN MANY GUISES

Peculiar ways to become threatened.

Colourful Puffleg

There are plenty of ways to become extinct, it seems. Much as the overwhelming majority of rare birds are threatened primarily by habitat destruction, some face difficulties of quite different kinds. The examples in the following pages are a sample of the more unusual threats that are presently afflicting birds.

Several species down the years have met their demise by bizarre happenstance. Perhaps the most famous concerns the tale of the Stephens Island Wren (*Xenicus lyalli*), a minute bird that only lived on its eponymous small island in the Cook Strait, between New Zealand's North Island and South Island. It seems to have met its end by being predated by a very small group of cats, introduced to the island in 1894. It became extinct within a year.

Another unfortunate species was the Wake Island Rail (*Gallirallus wakensis*) which, once again, just inhabited a small area, two islands in an atoll in the North Pacific. In 1941, Japanese soldiers occupied the island but three years later their supply route was cut, leaving them trying to survive off the land. Within a year they had eaten the rail to extinction – meaning that the rail became the only known avian casualty of World War II.

Several other well-known extinctions have an unexpected element. For example, some of the native birds on Hawaii have been partly driven to extinction by getting malaria from introduced mosquitoes. And the Great Auk (*Pinguinus impennis*) could potentially still be alive today had one of its main breeding islands, Geirfuglasker, not sunk beneath the sea in a volcanic explosion in 1830.

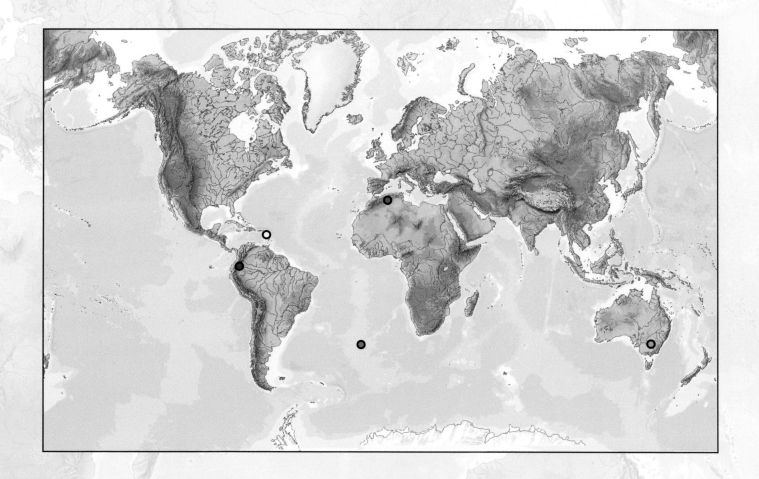

TRISTAN ALBATROSS

Diomedea debbenena

David eradicating Goliath?

The Tristan Albatross must suffer from one of the most bizarre threats faced by any species in the world. Despite it being one of the largest and most powerful birds of all, a close relative of the huge Wandering Albatross (*Diomedea exulans*) with its record-breaking wingspan (up to 3.6m), it seems that the Tristan Albatross's fluffy young are at constant risk from being attacked and eaten by giant mice. Yes, you have read it correctly – mice.

If you find this hard to believe, imagine the feelings of Richard Cuthbert and Ross Wanless, who were the first to observe the grisly mouse attacks in 2004, when they captured them on video. Although it was suspected for some time that rodents were a problem to the seabird chicks of Gough Island, in the South Atlantic, it still must have come as a shock to watch the gruesome execution happen before your eyes. 'Once one mouse has attacked a chick,' says Wanless, from the University of Cape Town's Percy Fitzpatrick Institute, 'the blood seems to attract others. They

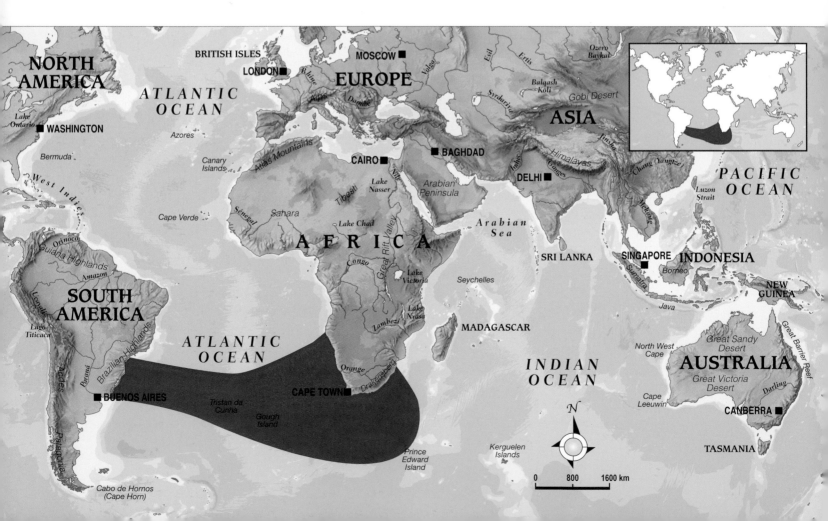

Above: A Tristan Albatross sails over the volcanic peaks of Gough Island, the key breeding station for the species.

gnaw into the chick's body, create a gaping wound and the chick weakens then dies over several days.' In scenes reminiscent of the worst horror movie, up to 10 mice have been observed gradually killing a single young albatross, allowing it to bleed to death or for its vital organs to fail. It must be a truly horrendous way to die.

The truth is that strange things happen on islands. Gough Island is one of the Tristan da Cunha group, one of the most isolated archipelagos in the world. It is 2,700 km west of the nearest continental land mass, South Africa, in the midst of the South Atlantic Ocean. Its windswept, treeless moorland and tall cliffs hardly seem the most ideal rodent territory, but the indomitable House Mouse (*Mus domesticus*) was introduced to Gough by passing sailors some time in the 18th or 19th century and, being a tough survivor, it managed to cope with the exposure and rough climate, getting by any way it could. And, with over 10 million ground-nesting birds occurring here in the breeding season, it is perhaps not surprising that the local House Mice, those extraordinary opportunists,

started at length to turn to sinister nutritional ways. Along the way, it happens that these killers grew to be almost three times as heavy as 'normal' mice, weighing in at up to 40g instead of the usual 15g.

Even so, mouse versus albatross does seem to be an extraordinary mismatch. As Geoff Hilton, until 2008 like Cuthbert a researcher for Britain's Royal Society for the Protection of Birds, comments: 'It's remarkable that a 10kg albatross chick is vulnerable to attack by a 35g mouse; it's like a tabby cat attacking a hippopotamus.' The problem is, however, that for much of their early life the growing chicks, big though they are, are on their own. They take about nine months to fledge, and for much of that time are simply left at the nest site while the adults wander the oceans looking for food for them. Just a few months old, they cannot fly or move away from the mice; they are completely vulnerable and helpless. They are well able to cope with bad weather and near

TRISTAN ALBATROSS
Diomedea debbenena

starvation, but have never adapted to the new menace on the island posed by at least 700,000 bloodthirsty rodents.

The degree of threat posed by the mice is extremely serious for the species as a whole. This is partly because Tristan Albatrosses don't occur anywhere else but in the Tristan da Cunha group. Almost the entire world population breeds on Gough Island, with a few pairs on Inaccessible Island. The small world breeding range has always kept numbers low and, with no more than about 3,000 pairs recorded breeding in any one year, it was always likely to be more vulnerable than many other seabirds.

The second problem is that the predation level on Gough is extremely high. It has been estimated that five times as many albatross chicks would fledge from the island every year if the mice were not there. In

the 2007-08 breeding season the Tristan Albatross recorded its worst breeding season ever; the 1,764 pairs breeding raised a mere 246 fledged chicks between them. With the albatross's traditionally low reproductive rate (they don't breed until at least six years old, and only once every other year), that is an unsustainable level of depredation.

Furthermore, the mouse problem isn't the only threat faced by the giant bird. In common with other albatrosses, plus large numbers of other seabirds, Tristan Albatrosses suffer from mortality at sea caused by the practice of commercial long-lining. This method of fishing, used abundantly in the South Atlantic, involves vessels trailing baited lines up to 100km behind them on the ocean. The baits are fixed on hooks (there may be 12,000 of them) which are designed to sink below the surface between floats,

Opposite: An immature Tristan Albatross at sea (with Northern Giant Petrels *Macronectes halli* and Great Shearwater *Puffinus gravis*). In common with all albatrosses, the population of this species suffers from the practice of long-line fishing.

Left: Closely related to the Wandering Albatross (and only considered a separate species since 2004), the Tristan Albatross has one of the longest wing-spans of any bird in the world, up to 3.5m. This is an immature. Birds don't breed until they are about eight years old, an age beyond the total life expectancy of most landbirds.

thus attracting the fish. The main problem of long-lining is that birds are attracted to the baits before they are laid in the water beyond the vessel's stern; the albatrosses that attempt to scavenge the baits get caught in the hooks, are pulled underwater as the line settles into place, and drown.

Throughout the world, it is estimated that one albatross dies every five minutes from coming into conflict with fisheries, either as a result of this long-lining or by becoming trapped in trawl nets or cables. Clearly, this is an alarming statistic, especially for birds that are adapted to breeding at a slow reproductive rate. As a result, all albatrosses are classed as threatened and there is a real chance that they could disappear completely worldwide as common birds of the oceans. As for the Tristan Albatross, this species really cannot afford any extra

losses from long-lining, especially since the at-sea deaths incorporate all age classes, including breeding birds. With the twin threats facing it, the Tristan Albatross is currently classified as Critically Endangered.

The recent proof that mice are killing albatrosses attracted a good deal of press coverage, with all the usual ghoulish headlines you might expect. And in a way, perhaps this very quirk of predation will be the albatross's salvation. The British government, which administers the Tristan da Cunha group, has hitherto shown scant regard for the conservation of this isolated protectorate. Perhaps the very quirkiness of the story will invigorate enough interest in the snoozing minstries for them to find some money to eradicate the mice and provoke the odd favourable headline.

BLACK-EARED MINER
Manorina melanotis

the Black-eared Miner's specialized habitat, or the modification of other parts, is what set in train the unfortunate hybridization clash between the two species.

The Yellow-throated Miner is a relatively unspecialized bird occurring in various types of open eucalyptus woodland right cross the continent of Australia. The Black-eared Miner, on the other hand, is much more fussy ecologically, being confined to a biome known as mallee, a community of small (less than 6m tall), multi-stemmed eucalypts with woody underground root systems that grows in semi-arid parts of southern Australia. The Black-eared Miner has always occurred in the denser, large tracts of mallee that had not been disrupted by fire or other clearing factors for at least 20 years, and it was this preference that had kept it isolated from its counterpart. However, from the early 20th century European settlers cleared substantial areas of mallee to make way for agriculture. At the same time they dug drains and dammed rivers and, together with other modifications, this opened up other parts of the mallee and fragmented them, allowing in populations of Yellow-throated Miners which flourished along the margins. As soon as the populations met, the introgression of Yellow-throated Miner genes began to compromise Black-eared Miners. It was, therefore, the destruction and then alteration of core habitat that drove the Black-eared Miner to its decline, a story that has a depressingly familiar ring to it.

Before long the Black-eared Miner was known to be in serious trouble. In fact, as recently as 1995 only 28 pure-bred birds were known to exist in the wild. Had that situation persisted the species would surely have disappeared, but between 1996 and 2002 a relatively large population was discovered in Bookmark Biosphere Reserve in South Australia. Thorough monitoring unearthed a population of 3,758 pure adults, as well as 2,255 hybrids. The known population in Murray Sunset National Park in Victoria numbered 53 birds, including hybrids, at around the same time.

For most species a population of 3,758 pure adults in one place, even if mixed with hybrids, might give some cause for optimism. However, there is another interesting quirk of the Black-eared Miner's biology that makes these bald figures much less encouraging. In common with the other miners in Australia, including the intensively studied Noisy Miner (*Manorina melanocephala*), the Black-eared Miner is a co-operatively breeding species in which only a limited number of individuals contribute genetically to each nesting attempt. Within a given colony, which may contain a few to about 20 birds, there may only be one or two nests but up to 13 helpers, usually males, which contribute to feeding the breeding female's chicks. The sex ratio is strongly favoured towards males (1.8 to 1) and in one colony it was discovered that 81 per cent of females breed in a given season and only 14 per cent of males. All in all, the experts have worked out that the viable population of Black-eared Miners at Bookmark Reserve is only 390 pure-bred birds, along with 234 hybrids, or only about a tenth of the total population.

With such a small and easily sullied gene pool, the future of the Black-eared Miner is therefore still looking extremely uncertain. And, of course, with its reduced population, the wild stock is also extremely

vulnerable to catastrophic events such as wildfires. In 2006 a fire at Bookmark destroyed 115,000ha of the miners' habitat, and there is little that can be done to ensure that this doesn't happen again. Indeed, the effect of this fire on the population has still not yet been quantified.

In 1996 a small number of Black-eared Miners was take from the wild to begin a captive breeding programme. It still persists today, and in 2003 45 birds were released in Victoria; evidence suggests that at least one or two of these individuals have bred, or at least taken part in a breeding attempt.

For many years the Black-eared Miner was only doubtfully considered as a separate species from its near relative, the Yellow-throated Miner, and indeed there are many today that still question whether sustained efforts should be made to save such a genetically similar and compromised bird. However, recent studies of the mitochondrial DNA have confirmed the view that the Black-eared Miner is best treated as a full species. And besides, when birds are separated by small nuances of behaviour and habitat, surely that is just cause to celebrate biodiversity at its cutting edge.

MONTSERRAT ORIOLE

Icterus oberi

Down in flames

Such is the long litany of grievances that can be made against humankind on behalf of endangered birds, it is almost a relief to come across a species that is not currently imperilled by our activities. So it's of interest – albeit not very pleasing – to report that the Montserrat Oriole is Critically Endangered – but because of natural forces.

This smart-looking bird, with its combination of yellow-orange and black plumage, is endemic to its namesake island, in the Leeward Islands of the Caribbean. Montserrat is a mere 104km² in extent, so the population of its only endemic species, the Montserrat Oriole, has always been commensurately small. Historically, however, Montserrat has escaped the worst excesses of deforestation or overgrazing, as have many tropical islands worldwide, and some reasonably intact forest cover remained on the slopes above the lowlands, providing the core habitat of the oriole. And while the conservation agencies were keeping a careful watch on the species, there was little alarm that its survival might be at stake.

All that changed in 1989 when Montserrat was struck by the first of a double whammy of natural disasters. Hurricane Hugo ravaged the island in September of that year, wiping out much of the economy and felling large numbers of trees. As far as the orioles were concerned, it is notoriously difficult to measure the effects of such natural disasters on wild birds, but it seems common sense that the oriole's numbers must have been reduced, since the birds are known to be adversely affected by heavy rain. Then, in July 1995, towards the end of the orioles' breeding season, there was a far more devastating event. Mount Soufriere erupted for the first time in recorded history and covered large parts of the island with mud and ash. The capital, Plymouth, was completely wiped out, 12m under the mud. And much of the Montserrat Oriole's prime habitat was also destroyed within a few days.

A large volcanic eruption on such a small island could easily have wiped out all of the local orioles. Pyroclastic flows, which are lethal currents of hot gas and rock that travel down from the volcanic summit at up to 700km per hour, and may reach 1,000°C, did

Left: The Montserrat Oriole is a forest bird that usually sticks to the high canopy. This bird has been colour-ringed as part of a monitoring programme.

wipe out large areas of forest and killed everything in their path. At the same time much of Montserrat was covered in hot ash, seriously compromising the birds' ability to find food. However, fortunately the very worst effects were confined to the south side of the island, leaving the northern half at least inhabitable, and it soon became clear that some of the orioles had survived the initial impact.

Before the eruption the orioles were found in three areas, the Centre Hills, the Soufriere Hills and the South Soufriere Hills, and fieldworkers soon went out to these areas in search of them. It was obvious that, at a stroke, the Soufriere birds were wiped out, and no trace of them was found on the charred hillsides or in the fields of ash. There seemed little hope for the South Soufriere birds, either, since they occurred close to the area most affected by the eruption. However, remarkably, a small group also managed to hold on in a small relict tract of forest only 1km from the summit of the volcano and these, together with the Centre Hills population, held a decent pool of surviving birds.

However, the initial eruption was only the beginning of the Montserrat Oriole's problems. The next, and very serious threat, was habitat alteration. The Montserrat Oriole is unusual within its family (the American blackbirds, or Icteridae), in being very much a forest bird, shunning the edge habitats more typical of many of its relatives. Before the eruption it

MONTSERRAT ORIOLE
Icterus oberi

had been confined mainly to slopes above 460m with a lush growth of palms, filmy ferns and epiphytes, where it fed mainly by gleaning foliage in the higher canopy. Now it was faced with surviving in forest with an ash-covered understorey, and living in a drier environment. It also differed from its relatives in its food, largely forsaking such mainstays as fruit or nectar in the wild in favour of a strict invertebrate diet. Such quirks were not likely to make recovery easy. Birds found it difficult to forage, and others are thought to have become ill.

Nevertheless, the birds did hold on in both their fragile refuges, despite their whole world range being limited to 10km² of forest. For the next few years they showed a decline of 40–50 per cent, down to approximately 2,000 individuals. Population modelling predicted that the species had a 50 per cent chance of becoming extinct within 10 years. Then, unfortunately, in 2001 there was another eruption of Mount Soufriere, spewing hot ash over the forest again. A number of nests were destroyed – these, incidentally, are splendid hanging-baskets woven with vegetation and suspended from the lower leaves of a heliconia, or sometimes a banana tree – and breeding

Opposite: Montserrat is a hilly, relatively unspoilt island in the Caribbean. Unfortunately, it is also volcanic.

Left: Much of the oriole's habitat is now protected.

Below: For a bright bird the Montserrat Oriole can be hard to find. It lives at low density in forest and, for a songbird, is unusually quiet, even in the breeding season.

was abandoned for an entire season. The same thing happened in 2003 and again in 2006. The oriole's foothold on existence was slipping.

Since then, further problems have exacerbated the already critical situation. Nesting success – already low for this species, which only lays 2–3 eggs in a clutch – began to decline further. Nest cameras revealed that some nests were being raided by Black Rats (*Rattus rattus*) or by predatory Pearly-eyed Thrashers (*Margarops fuscatus*), a small bird related to the mockingbirds (Mimidae), while drought also affected the species, which prefers moist

environments. To add to these problems, the population of feral pigs began to increase in the Centre Hills, seriously compromising the forest habitat.

Under siege in its native land, the Montserrat Oriole continues to flirt with extinction. There is a healthy captive population which breeds well and will doubtless prevent the species from completely dying out, but what future does the bird have on its native island? In common with much of the human population that was forced to leave Montserrat forever after the 1995 eruption, the answer could well be: not much.

HOUBARA BUSTARD

Chlamydotis undulata

Hunted in the desert

The Houbara Bustard is a large, regally walking, ground-dwelling bird that lives in arid environments in North Africa. Like a miniature Ostrich (*Struthio camelus*), it spends its time patrolling the earth, picking up a mixture of seeds and invertebrates (especially grasshoppers and locusts), with the occasional snake or lizard thrown in. In common with the Ostrich, it usually escapes danger on foot; but unlike the Ostrich it can also fly, if necessary for great distances.

At almost all times of the year, the Houbara Bustard is a barely visible part of its harsh, open environment.

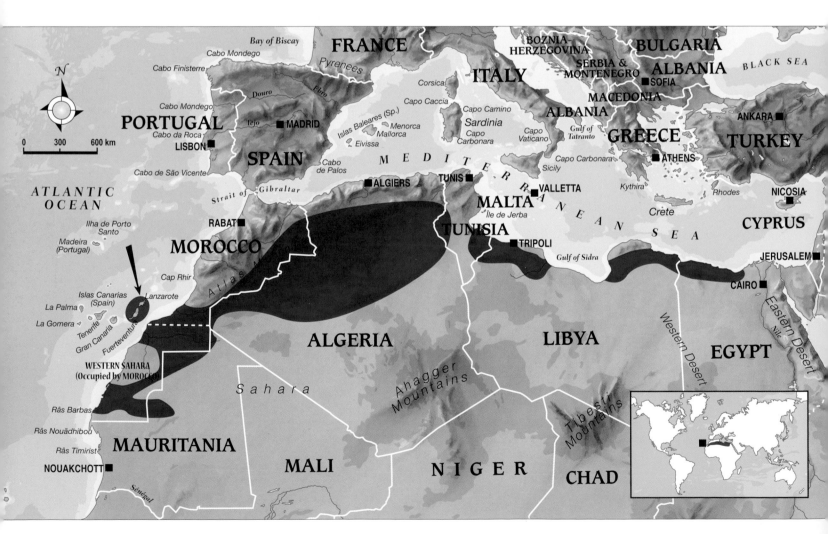

Left: The intricately patterned plumage of the Houbara Bustard makes it incredibly difficult to spot in the desert landscape.

Clad in subtle light brown with darker bars, and with a black stripe on its neck to disrupt the natural contours of its body, it can be almost impossible to see. Its behaviour completes the camouflage; it is exceedingly wary and furtive, and utterly silent. Only briefly, when in display, does it become conspicuous. Then the male Houbaras expose previously hidden white plumes from the neck and crown and ruffle them until they cover the whole head and neck; thus attired, the bird runs forward in measured high-steps, sometimes hitting obstacles in its blinded but highly excited state. Once it has copulated with one or more females, it returns to its retiring ways.

You might think that such an inoffensive bird, living in remote, hostile environments over a large range would be immune to many of the pressures faced by birds around the world. However, the Houbara has been singled out, if you will, for a particular and very personal persecution. It happens to be the quarry of choice for Arab falconers, from the Atlantic coast to the edge of the Nile. And as a result, numbers are tumbling almost everywhere.

Of course, there is an easy solution to this: just stop the falconers persecuting Houbaras. But there are powerful cultural forces at play here. The Houbara, the falcon and the desert play an emotional part in the Arab identity and way of life, and there is no immediate prospect of earning the Houbaras a complete reprieve. It is thought that falconry, as a sport, has been around in the Middle East for several millennia, and today no less than 50 per cent of all the world's falconers come from the Middle East. The sport, in which the birds of prey are trained over many years to catch food in the wild and bring it back

HOUBARA BUSTARD
Chlamydotis undulata

to their owners, is ingrained in many Arab cultures. Ancient Arab poets lauded falcons and falconry, and there is a mention of the sport in the Koran. All in all, that is quite a tradition.

However, in recent years methods of hunting have changed. The tradition of falconry, in which winter hunting parties would proceed by camel into remote areas, was once used to teach and demonstrate self-reliance and patience. However, gone are the days when man was pitted against Houbara in a tough contest in an extreme environment, with a fair chance for either. Nowadays some Arab hunting parties use luxury, desert-adapted vehicles instead of camels. They use back-up fleets with petrol tankers

Opposite: Having feathers in front of your face is awkward for a display posture. Excited birds frequently trip and run into obstacles.

Left: A displaying Houbara Bustard seems to turn itself inside out.

instead of having to be careful with the distances they travel, and they have cold showers and ready food rather than relying on roughing it. They use teams of falcons instead of one or two. And they use modern rifles in case the falcons have an off-day. They might be linking with their ancestors and their past in spirit, but they do it in a distinctly 21st century manner.

Of course, the Houbara Bustards suffer against this onslaught. There is no fairness. The hunters can clear an area of Houbaras in a matter of weeks. These days the birds might not even be eaten, their corpses just being left in piles to rot. Today the slaughter can be wholesale and unsustainable.

Hearing this, you might conclude that the Houbara's days will soon be numbered, but happily this scenario has not yet been reached. The Houbara is highly mobile and, most importantly, fits into some habitats that are so remote that not even the most determined hunting parties are likely to go there. However, the Houbaras are definitely declining, at the mercy not just of hunters but of habitat destruction and degradation and, in some areas of their range, from collisions with powerlines. In all, it is estimated

that their population has declined by about 25 per cent over the last 20 years.

Nevertheless, nobody really knows what the population of this North African species is; the terrain is very difficult, the research needed is extremely expensive, and until recently, at least, the security problems were prohibitive. Perhaps it is in danger of extinction; perhaps not. At least the conservation agencies should keep an eye on it.

Meanwhile, measures are being undertaken to alleviate the problems of hunting Houbara Bustards. Several private projects have sprung up in various Arab countries to breed the birds in captivity and then release these, to relieve the pressure on wild birds. In Morocco a major facility now does this within the range of the species, bolstering the regional population by many thousands a year. Although much of the stock involved in these projects comes from eggs taken in the wild, some of the birds, ironically, were caught to order, using age-old methods. They may have been hooded and their claws neutralized by adhesive beads, but falcons were used to catch the Houbaras – for conservation.

COLOURFUL PUFFLEG

Eriocnemis mirabilis

A small world for a small bird

You've probably never heard of the Colourful Puffleg, because it is pretty obscure. It is a hummingbird found only in the Andes of Colombia, in South America. It was only discovered in 1967 and almost nothing is known about it. Recently, however, it has found itself on the Critically Endangered list.

In many ways the Colourful Puffleg represents quite a number of bird species in the world. These are the ones which seem to have very small natural ranges, and as such can be plunged towards extinction by remarkably localized events. In the case of the Colourful Puffleg that range has been estimated as a mere 31km². In a part of the world where deforestation is rampant, that precious 31km² is very vulnerable.

After its 1967 discovery, at a place called Cerro Charguayaco in Munchique National Park in the south-west of Colombia, apart from one sighting this delightful hummingbird was pretty much ignored by birders (who probably hadn't realized what a stunner it is) until 1997, when it was rediscovered at exactly the same place. A study shortly afterwards made trips out from the type locality at a radius of 3km at various elevations, but never found the hummingbird more than 300m from its favoured location, and it was thought possibly to have the smallest range of any bird in the world. However, more recently it has been unearthed at three other sites.

To understand why the Colourful Puffleg has such a limited range, you have to appreciate some of the basics of Andean biogeography. These mountains are not a single chain, of course, but a parallel set of chains. On each slope of the three north–south chains different conditions apply, owing to variations in the moisture loads in the winds as they cross the mountains, creating different vegetation types. Now add altitude into the mix. The habitat at sea level will be quite different to the habitat at 7,000m and, focusing in, there will also be a quite different flora between, for example, 1,000m and 3,000m. If you then mix in rivers and other topographical features, and

Left: The strange feather tufts above the legs give the group of hummingbirds known as pufflegs its name. A rare gem of a hummer, the Colourful Puffleg was only discovered as recently as 1967.

take account of the effects of glaciation, it becomes easy to see how Colombia manages to hold more bird species than anywhere else on earth. But it also enables you to understand that, with very specific conditions occurring very locally, different species can be confined to small areas.

That what seems to have happened in the case of the Colourful Puffleg. It occurs in the western Andean range. It appears to occur only at altitudes between 2,200m and 2,600m (possibly higher), and it is a bird of wet forest. With intense competition from other hummingbirds in the same area, it seems to feed

COLOURFUL PUFFLEG
Eriocnemis mirabilis

mostly low down, between 2m and 4m above the ground. Thus it has a very narrow niche even within its strictly localized range.

All this, naturally, is a recipe for trouble. One day environmental pressures were almost bound to come calling, and at the moment these pressures are seriously threatening the tiny population of less than a thousand individuals. Up until the 1970s the local economy of the people was based on a fruit crop called 'lulo' which was grown under the forest canopy. However, in the 1980s there was a disaster: the lulo plants were hit by a double-whammy of fungal infection and pest infestation, and the cash crop collapsed. With no incentive to keep the forest, it began to be cleared. In other, newly discovered parts of the bird's range, forests were cleared to make way for coca production, even though this is completely illegal and inside the boundaries of a national park. Little by little, but inexorably, the Colourful Puffleg's habitat is diminishing.

The sheer small scale of this disaster needs to be recognized. The whole population of the Colourful Puffleg is confined to less than the area of, perhaps, a large town or small city. The loss of the lulo was a local event not much bigger than the closing of an employer in that same town. Upon such minimal

Opposite: Cloud-forest in Munchique National Park, the headquarters of the Colourful Puffleg.

Below: The Colourful Puffleg is just one of a number of hummingbirds with very small world ranges. Here it shows off its myriad colours and 'puff legs' to their full effect.

matters does the fate of a whole species of bird hang.

Interestingly, the Colourful Puffleg is not alone in having the difficult starting point of an abnormally small range. There are other birds in the world in similar difficulties. The most obvious candidates are island species, but continental endemics do occur. Several also happen to be hummingbirds, and another is a puffleg, the Black-breasted Puffleg (*Eriocnemis nigrivestis*), which only occurs in a small part of neighbouring Ecuador. It is both a worry and a wonder. The wonder is that so many species have evolved in such small areas with such exacting parameters. The worry, of course, is how vulnerable these treasures are.

AQUATIC WARBLER

Acrocephalus paludicola

A bird full of surprises

The Aquatic Warbler is a small, brown, streaky bird that breeds mostly in eastern Europe. For a small brown bird it has a pretty extraordinary lifestyle, both behaviourally and ecologically; and for a European bird it has a fascinating history, which includes two crucial recent discoveries. It is currently the continent's rarest breeding songbird, with a total maximum population of 14,200 singing males, 80 per cent of which are found at only four sites. Overall, it is listed as Vulnerable.

The Aquatic Warbler's mating system, only comparatively recently described, is highly unusual. In most other small birds, the partnership between a male and female assumes that both sexes will play defined roles, and in males this is usually a significant contribution towards feeding the young. In Aquatic Warblers this isn't the case at all; the males do nothing whatsoever, and the females do all the chick-rearing. The reason for the male's emancipation seems to be that Aquatic Warbler's specialized habitat is so rich in

Below: The Aquatic Warbler is exceptionally fussy in its habitat requirements on both its breeding and wintering grounds.

insects that it is easy for the female to be the sole provider.

This leaves the males with little to do except to defend a territory and fight tooth and nail for sexual access to females, leading to intense sperm competition, in which every male competes with every other male for any female in the immediate vicinity of its territory. One result of this is that about 59 per cent of all Aquatic Warbler broods are fathered by more than one male, and often more. Indeed, a few clutches of six eggs are known to have been fathered by five different males. Another unusual result of the free-for-all is that, in the Aquatic Warbler, copulation can last for an extraordinary amount of time: while in most small birds it lasts a fraction of a second, in Aquatic Warblers it can drag on for as long

AQUATIC WARBLER
Acrocephalus paludicola

as 30 minutes – anything to keep competing males away.

However, as noted above, this strange arrangement comes at a price: the habitat for breeding birds must be rich enough for lone parenting to work, for the female to raise its brood successfully. For an Aquatic Warbler, it seems, the requirements are exacting. The site must be a wetland dominated by clumps of sedge to a maximum of 80cm tall, and there must be standing water between the clumps somewhere between 1cm and 10cm deep. Not surprisingly, such habitats are at a premium, and in these days when so many wetlands have disappeared and are still disappearing, the number of sites holding breeding Aquatic Warblers has declined alarmingly. The species once occurred commonly in Western Europe, including France, Belgium, Italy and the Netherlands, but it is now extinct as a breeder in all these countries, mainly because of habitat destruction for agriculture and peat extraction. It is struggling in Germany, and the tiny population that used to occur in west Siberia is probably also extinct. The species now only persists as a regular breeder in six countries: Germany, Poland, Lithuania, Hungary, Ukraine and Belarus.

In fact, the current population is much higher than was estimated a few years ago. One of the crucial discoveries mentioned above was the finding of a major breeding population in the under-watched country of Belarus in the mid-1990s. Indeed, breeding populations unearthed since 1995 account for no less than two-thirds of all the Aquatic Warblers now known in the world. It seems extraordinary that a bird virtually confined to Europe would have been previously so poorly known.

However, the problems of the Aquatic Warbler don't finish with finding a place to breed. In common with most species of warblers in the world's temperate zones, the Aquatic Warbler is a migrant, making a long journey to its wintering grounds each year. Somewhat awkwardly, this species also uses important staging areas where it typically halts its migration to refuel; the majority are thought to use estuaries in northern France, where the birds feed up and gain weight before making a single long flight to West Africa. This means that not only do its wintering grounds need to be protected, but so also do these stop-off points. And, inevitably, the Aquatic Warbler is fussy wherever it goes, requiring strongly inundated marshlands and fens. It is a high-maintenance, conservation-dependent species.

Until recently however, no plan of action for the Aquatic Warbler's welfare was in any way adequate, because although the species was known to migrate to Africa, nobody had any idea exactly where. In the winter of 2007, however, this pressing puzzle was solved – and in elegant style, through a combination of high science and traditional fieldwork. Researchers from the Aquatic Warbler Conservation Team took feathers from warblers ringed in Europe, and they then subjected them to isotope analysis. Isotopes are variations of elements, such as hydrogen, carbon or strontium, which are found naturally in the environment. When a bird feeds it absorbs isotopes and, if it is growing feathers, an isotope signature will be preserved within the inert keratin that makes up the feather structure. It so happens that various parts of the world have distinctive isotope profiles, as do different habitats and climates, and it is possible to

Left: It was some remarkable ground-breaking scientific research, coupled with carefully targeted fieldwork, that finally uncovered the secret location of the Aquatic Warbler's wintering grounds in Senegal, where this bird is being ringed.

map the presence of isotopes for any part of the world quite accurately. Thus, by analysing feathers and comparing them to your map, you can tell roughly where a bird has been.

In this way the Conservation Team narrowed down their search for Aquatic Warbler wintering sites to a zone just south of the Sahara Desert and, by using the few previous records from the general area, decided to check the immediate vicinity of the Senegal River. With a great deal of hard graft, they located the birds, in an area of about 100km² within the Djoudj National Park in Senegal. The area is estimated to hold up to 10,000 birds, a very significant proportion of the world population. Doubtless with further study and effort, the team will find the rest.

There is no doubt that the Aquatic Warbler's future looks a good deal brighter now than it did only 10 or 15 years ago. Its reversal in fortunes is down to good conservation efforts, backed up by excellent research. However, it would not take much to tip the species back into danger, especially in the vulnerable habitats that it uses everywhere it goes.

NORDMANN'S GREENSHANK

Tringa guttifer

A weird and wonderful wader

There is nothing particularly unusual about the appearance of Nordmann's Greenshank. To many it just looks like any other shorebird or wader. Even to enthusiasts it is pretty similar to the widespread Common Greenshank (*Tringa nebularia*) and can only be identified with care. It is not the sort of bird to stand out from the crowd.

In terms of its behaviour, however, Nordmann's Greenshank is distinctly unusual. It seems, for example, that it builds its own nest. Lest you were underwhelmed by this fact – don't birds build nests? – consider that this is a shorebird, and shorebirds don't usually do very much more than make a shallow scrape in the ground and lay eggs in that. But it seems that Nordmann's Greenshank constructs a large nest from larch twigs, moss and hanging lichens, collecting some of its material from the ground and pulling twigs from the trees. And while virtually every other shorebird is ground-dwelling, Nordmann's Greenshank puts its impressive construction up in the branches of larches, between 2.3m and 4.5m above the ground. This means, of course, that when the four chicks hatch one of their first tasks in life is to jump to the ground.

Another quirk of Nordmann's Greenshank's breeding life is that it forms solidly monogamous pair-bonds. Again this might seem far from earth-shattering, but in the context of shorebirds it is, once again, notable. Migrant shorebirds that breed in the far north often form loose pair-bonds that lead to multiple partners, and often a single-parent upbringing for the chicks. But Nordmann's Greenshank pairs stay together, not just to build the nest, but also to incubate the eggs and look after the chicks as well, taking them to nearby marshes to catch small fish and aquatic invertebrates.

Nordmann's Greenshank is altogether something of a mysterious species. It is certainly rare and localized. It only breeds in the Russian Far East, on Sakhalin Island and by the Sea of Okhotsk to the north, where it selects a fairly specialized habitat incorporating swamps, larch forests and nearby coastal bays with mudflats. Few people have ever seen it on its breeding grounds, and it has probably always been sparsely

Below: At first glance it might look like an unremarkable bird, but the Nordmann's Greenshank exhibits some very strange behavioural traits for a wader.

NORDMANN'S GREENSHANK
Tringa guttifer

distributed. After breeding it departs in July and August (adults) or September (juveniles) to make its way to wintering grounds over a broad area of southern Asia. However, neither its migration routes nor the extent of its wintering grounds are yet fully understood.

And this causes a problem. With a population estimate of less than 1,000 individuals, and perhaps as few as 500, it is important that conservationists know all about Nordmann's Greenshank's whereabouts and needs. It is known that it likes tidal mudflats, where it can indulge in its passion for crabs, but large swathes of habitat which might be suitable for it remain unused. The other problem is the large number of

countries in which it has been reported in the non-breeding season: South Korea, China, Bangladesh, Malaysia, much of the rest of South-East Asia; even Guam, Australia, the Philippines and, bizarrely, Nepal. Why it goes to certain places at certain times is far from clear, and this makes working out how to conserve the species tricky. Some of the more consistent wintering sites include Bangladesh and Malaysia, in the latter of which 146 birds were found recently in four different locations. And as far as migration stopovers are concerned, Nordmann's Greenshank is known regularly to pass through China (the celebrated Mai Po wetland in Hong Kong, for example) and South Korea.

What has become clear about this wanderer, however, is that its future does not look particularly healthy. On the breeding grounds some of its habitat is being degraded by grazing Reindeer (*Rangifer tarandus*). Only recently a crucial stopover site, Saemangeum in South Korea, was recklessly destroyed by development, and a similar picture is being drawn all over southern Asia, where coastal mudflats are often the targets for reclamation. The truth is that, by having separate breeding, migrating and wintering areas, Nordmann's Greenshank is a high-maintenance species, but that does not make its needs any less important than those of a sedentary rarity. Indeed, a great deal of the appeal of shorebirds is down to their extensive migrations and often, their unpredictability.

You might look at a Nordmann's Greenshank in among thousands of other shorebirds in its drab winter plumage and wonder what all the fuss is about. But if you look harder you will see that it has different

Opposite: Many of Southern Asia's muddy estuaries are severely threatened. This is Samut Sakhan, close to Bangkok in Thailand, which has held small numbers of the species during winter in recent years.

Above: The two-toned, heavy bill, short legs and bulky body all distinguish this non-breeding bird from the more widespread Common Greenshank (*Tringa nebularia*).

ways of doing things from the others. It will catch a crab – anywhere between 5cm and 40cm across – and, if it is large, simply shake it violently until the legs fall off, upon which it will swallow its victim piecemeal. Another trait is to run fast through the shallow water will its bill down, chasing fish.

Nordmann's Greenshank will never be a headline-grabber, attracting vast sums of money to relieve its plight. Its delight is in its subtle differences to related birds, its celebration of the niceties of biodiversity. In a way a bird like this is a yardstick, a measure of just how much we want to preserve the less glamorous species with which we share our planet.

NORTHERN BALD IBIS

Geronticus eremita

Migrants and pilgrims

It can be hard to be optimistic about the fortunes of a bird that has been in decline for several hundred years. It's a very long period over which to report losses in population and contraction in range. Yet for the Northern Bald Ibis, resignation over its future has cautiously given way in the last few years to a new flicker of optimism. After a seemingly endless trough, its story in the last 30 years has become a truly compelling one.

Nobody is quite sure when the Northern Bald Ibis had its heyday. It appears on Egyptian hieroglyphs

dated from 5,000 years ago. It used to breed in the heart of Europe, with records from Switzerland, Austria, Germany, former Yugoslavia and Hungary, and was present at least to the end of the 16th or 17th centuries. It almost certainly occurred in other parts of Europe, although there is no proof. We can assume, though, that it was reasonably common and widespread in Europe, North Africa and the Middle East up until some 400 or 500 years ago.

Nobody is quite sure either why it disappeared from many of these places, but it most surely did. No

doubt it was shot for food, and suffered from the reclamation of the meadows, steppes and hillsides where it lived and fed on crickets, grasshoppers, beetles, frogs and lizards. It was easily disturbed on the dry cliffs or steep boulder slopes on which it nested. But this doesn't explain the whole picture. Perhaps large rafts of the population died from natural causes? We will never know.

What we can be sure of is that, in the 20th century, the Northern Bald Ibis accelerated its long-term decline. Soon all the known small outposts in Algeria and Syria disappeared, and the only viable colonies could be found in Turkey and Morocco. The colony at Birecik in Turkey, where the birds bred in cliffs just above the village, was especially important, and famous. It held at least 1,000 birds in 1911, and continued to thrive into the 1950s.

The story of the Birecik birds was intriguing. While the populations in Europe had been persecuted and destroyed, the birds here survived. Why? It was all because of their migratory habits. The breeding birds used to leave Birecik in August and return in early spring, when the locals held a festival to honour their return. It was believed that, when they left the area in the autumn, they guided Hajj pilgrims to Mecca down in the south. It was also believed that the Northern Bald Ibis had guided Noah after he had landed on

Top left: The Northern Bald Ibis usually breeds in small colonies on cliff ledges. Such sites are often traditional, and may be used for hundreds of years.

Above: Once occurring in the heart of Europe, the Northern Bald Ibis is now restricted to tiny breeding areas in Morocco and the Middle East. The reasons behind its long-term decline are a mystery.

NORTHERN BALD IBIS
Geronticus eremita

nearby Mount Ararat after the Biblical Flood. All in all, the Northern Bald Ibises of Birecik were much honoured.

The tradition of honouring the ibises in Turkey was all the more interesting because scientists didn't actually know where they went on their journey south. Flocks were regularly seen in Ethiopia and neighbouring Sudan from December to February, but their movements between August and December were unknown.

Unfortunately, reverence from people is not always

enough for a bird population and the Turkish population crashed in the second half of the 20th century. Between 1959 and 1960, over 600 Northern Bald Ibises were found dead close to Birecik, evidently the victims of unintentional pesticide poisoning in the fields where they fed. Tragically, by 1989 only a single wild bird from this population remained. Nevertheless, affection for the birds was such that a captive breeding population was established in 1977 and maintained a pool of local birds. When the wild birds disappeared, individuals from this group lived

Opposite: In contrast to most other members of its family, the Northern Bald Ibis often feeds in very dry areas, on such foods as crickets and lizards.

Left: The Middle Eastern population migrates to Ethiopia for the winter.

wild on the local cliffs for most of the year but, ironically, were caged in autumn to prevent them flying to their uncertain fate down south.

Meanwhile, by 1990 the only known wild breeding birds anywhere in the world were in Morocco. This population had suffered a slump, too, and there were now only two colonies left (there were 38 in 1940), both on the coast close to Agadir. In contrast to the Turkish birds, these individuals were not migratory, but remained in the country all year, making them easier to monitor and conserve. In 1991 one of the main strongholds, the Souss-Massa area on the coast close to Agadir, was designated a national park, and local people were enlisted into the effort to help and monitor the breeding birds. With this protection, the Souss-Massa birds and the large population slightly to the north, at Tamri, began to prosper. The last 10 years have seen the first increases in the wild population for perhaps half a millennium.

In 2002, against all expectations, the wild eastern population made a Phoenix-like reappearance. After tip-offs from Bedouin hunters, a tiny population was rediscovered at Palmyra in Syria; clearly, the Northern Bald Ibis had never disappeared from the country, and had indeed, by all accounts, been doing fine for the last 70 years until a recent crash in population. Now there were only two pairs and three subadult birds remaining, just at one site.

But this was better than nothing. Not only were the birds resilient, raising 24 young between 2002 and 2008, but the age-old question of the migratory whereabouts of the eastern population was also poised to be solved. The young ibises were duly fitted with transmitters so that their movements could be satellite-tracked.

The results so far have been most intriguing. The birds seem to go south through Jordan and Saudi Arabia before finding their way to Ethiopia. Some birds have also been recorded in Yemen and, excitingly, some untagged birds have recently been sighted in Israel and Djibouti, suggesting that there might yet be some unknown populations at large somewhere in the Middle East. Happily, the Birecik semi-wild colony, which numbers 150 birds, has now provided some young birds for reintroduction into the wild, and these have been shown to visit the colony at Palmyra.

These results have also proved something else. The birds from Birecik, if they did follow the same route as the wild Syrian birds, would indeed have passed right by the town of Mecca, in Saudi Arabia. It seems that the locals have been right all along.

KIRTLAND'S WARBLER

Dendroica kirtlandii

The world's fussiest species?

It's always a shock to see TV news items about wildfires, anywhere in the world. Ever graphic, they show frightening shots of huge flames, detail the human losses and usually feature long pans across charred landscapes that once were lush and verdant. The overall message is that fires kill, maim and destroy – they are a bad thing.

But this is a very simplistic view and, at least in an ecological sense, it can be quite wrong. Some habitats require regular burning in order to remain as they are, keeping them from becoming overgrown and modified into dense woodland. Some plant seeds, indeed, will not germinate unless a fire has passed by. And it follows that, for a few specialized creatures, regular wildfires are their lifeblood; without the occasional inferno, they would simply become extinct.

One of these curious specialists is counted among North America's rarest birds. Kirtland's Warbler has one of the smallest continental breeding ranges of any species in the world. At best it only covers about 516km², and at times has only occupied 18km² of the world's surface. Virtually the whole breeding area is within the US state of Michigan, although the species is also occasionally found in neighbouring parts of Canada. Interestingly, there is scant evidence that it has ever been very much more numerous than it is now. It is the epitome of a naturally rare species. And this paucity is explained by a quite astonishing aspect of its ecology: it is about as fussy as it is possible to be.

Right: Breeding regularly in just one state of the USA, the number of Kirtland's Warblers has always been very low – perhaps never more than 3,000 individuals.

Kirtland's Warbler only breeds in stands of one particular tree, the Jack Pine (*Pinus banksiana*). For optimal habitat, the stands must be pure, and these usually grow on sandy soil. Furthermore, not every Jack Pine stand will do; the trees must be young, less than 15 years old, and their height must be between 2m and 4m. Anything more, and the structure of the woodland is no longer ideal for the bird's foraging and nesting activities. These, you might say, are exacting standards. There must also be other, poorly understood specifications, perhaps climatic, because the Jack Pine is quite a widespread tree of northern North America, and the birds live only in this small fraction of its range. So, all in all, Kirtland's Warbler is not the easiest ecological customer to satisfy.

Not surprisingly, numbers of Kirtland's Warblers have always been limited. The first official survey in 1951 recorded a mere 432 singing males in the world (and an unrecorded number of females). Since then, the population has sometimes teetered alarmingly towards extinction, for example in 1974 and 1987 when, on both occasions, only 167 singing males remained. Other years have seen much healthier numbers, for example in 2006 there were 1,478 singing males and the world population was estimated at 2,830 individuals. Recent trends have generally been encouraging, but the population of Kirtland's Warblers on the whole is still desperately vulnerable.

Part of the reason for the tense situation in 1974 is that people had failed to understand the need for regular fires in the area where the warblers bred. Jack Pine is an unusual tree that needs burning for its regeneration; when a blaze passes, the older,

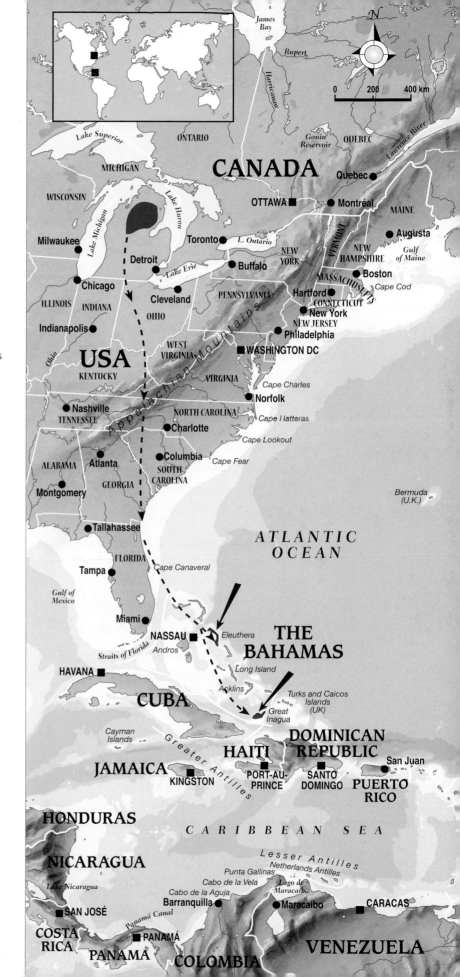

WHOOPING CRANE

Grus americana

Following a microlight to safety

The story of bird conservation down the years is littered with the heroic deeds, determination and innovation of individuals who wished to make a difference to the natural world. But few stories can match the sheer ambition, technological expertise and pure chutzpah of the current efforts to help save the Whooping Crane.

There's no doubt that the Whooping Crane is the epitome of a flagship species. It is North America's tallest bird, with striking white plumage and a truly magnificent flight-style, with slow, regal wing-beats. It has been a rarity for so long that it is probably more famous for its endangered status than for anything else. Anybody who takes even the slightest interest in birds in America knows that the Whooping Crane is close to extinction. So it is perhaps not surprising that great efforts and expense have been made on its behalf; it would be a very public and cultural tragedy if it were to disappear.

The story of the bird's decline follows the usual familiar pattern of dozens of species worldwide. The Whooping Crane used to occur in wetlands amidst the tall grass prairies of the American Midwest from Illinois to Alberta, although it was never especially

Below: A Whooping Crane in flight. Youngsters follow their parents on migration, and it is this quirk that has allowed captive-bred birds to be taught new routes.

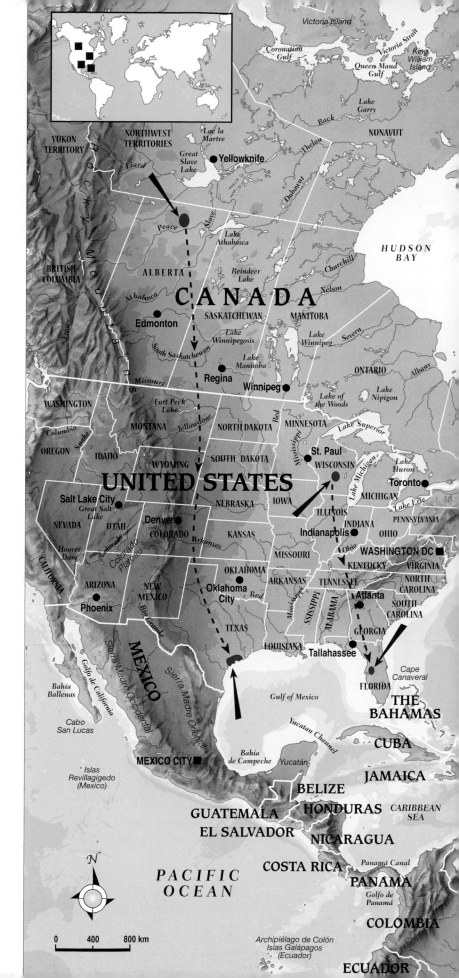

numerous, with a maximum population of perhaps 10,000 birds. It soon became a victim of a drive to put the grasslands under the plough, vastly decreasing its available habitat, and at the same time it was highly sensitive to disturbance on its breeding grounds. To make matters worse it was regularly hunted and, by being large and conspicuous, was a relatively easy target for guns. It wasn't long before its population began to crash, and even by 1937 there were probably only 40 birds left.

The Whooping Crane's recovery is a well-known story. In 1941 there were just 15 or 16 birds left, in a migratory population that bred in a remote part of the boreal forest of Canada, on the border between Alberta and the Northwest Territories, and wintered on the Texas coast. By acquiring legal protection for the birds' sole breeding grounds at Wood Buffalo National Park and their wintering site at Aransas, the first crucial steps were taken, and at the same time hunters were educated and urged not to shoot the birds. This stalled the decline and, little by little, the crane flock increased. It took a long time, but by increasing at about five per cent a year the Whooping Crane population has, over the last half-century, reached far more sustainable levels. In 2009 there were about 270 birds.

However, for a long time it has been recognized that this wild migratory population, although increasing, is very vulnerable to a single disaster, such as disease or a violent weather event. As long ago as 1967 it was decided to start breeding the birds in captivity. Single eggs from clutches of two found at the breeding site, at Wood Buffalo National Park in Canada, were brought to Patuxent Wildlife Research

WHOOPING CRANE
Grus americana

Center in Maryland and hatched in captivity. These efforts, which are still ongoing, have established populations numbering hundreds of birds, and if the wild population is hit by disaster, then at least there will be a pool of captive birds to preserve the species.

However, in recent years conservation visionaries have postulated that the best way to promote the survival of the Whooping Crane would be to establish a second population well away from the existing wild one. However, that is very much easier said than done. That it has been attempted at all, given the

difficulties, and that it has recently spawned some success, is a tribute to the sheer audacity of the project.

The idea, no less, has been to plant Whooping Cranes into new but suitable breeding and wintering areas – and to teach them to migrate between the two! It so happens that Whooping Cranes are unusual migrants. While most species of birds are born with their migration route in their head, cranes (and geese and some other wildfowl) learn theirs by following their parents – and once learned, it is remembered for

Opposite: A pair of Whooping Cranes. In 1941 these two birds would have constituted 12.5 per cent of the species' world population.

Left: At 1.5m, the elegant Whooping Crane is North America's tallest bird.

life. In theory, therefore, young cranes could be trained to follow a surrogate parent from one place to another.

A few years ago this would have been completely impossible. But since 2001, a non-profit organization called Operation Migration has brought in a resource which was not previously available – microlight aircraft. If young Whooping Cranes could be taught to follow a microlight, perhaps an unused migration route could be planted in their psyche?

To pull off this trick required an enormous amount of hard work and planning. First, new suitable breeding and wintering grounds were chosen, in Necedah, Wisconsin (a former breeding site), and at Chassahowitzka National Wildlife Refuge in Florida, two sites 2,500km apart. The chicks would be released at the former at the end of the breeding season and then, at the appropriate time, would commence their southbound migration following the microlight.

But how do you teach a Whooping Crane to follow a microlight aircraft? Well, first you raise the chick in isolation, something that is still done at Patuxent. The young birds are reared in enclosures and looked after by people dressed in Whooping Crane costume – they look a little bit like beekeepers, but use a hand puppet with the crane's distinctive red crown for more intimate contact, such as showing a chick where to

peck on the ground. Meanwhile, Whooping Crane calls are heard constantly – and there's another sound introduced soon, too, the sound of a microlight engine. When the chicks are old enough, somebody dressed in costume holding a large puppet with a long reach (known as 'Robo-crane') will walk alongside or get into the microlight, to give the chick an idea that it is a 'friend'. Later on, while the chicks are still in pens (to prevent injury), Robo-crane will begin to drive the microlight and encourage the youngster to run alongside. Little by little the chicks accept and follow the microlight. Before long, a microlight pilot dressed as a crane makes aerial passes overhead, while another handler releases the birds into a field. At first, the fledged Whooping Cranes simply hop around and flap their wings. But not long afterward, they habitually take flight and follow the machine.

Amazingly, this outlandish experiment has worked well. Indeed, at the first attempt, the young cranes did indeed follow the microlight from Wisconsin to Florida, wintered and some flew back again the same way. They took a long time to get from one place to another, with the plane constantly needing to land and refuel, but they did at least make it. And over the years, more and more Whooping Cranes have been released and the trick repeated. By 2009 there were about 80 birds in the new flock.

In 2006 there was a particularly special event. The first chick was raised in the wild in Wisconsin and migrated south, following its parents, who were graduates of the scheme, all the way to Florida.

Even if this never happened again, it was a tribute to those who dreamed of Whooping Cranes following a microlight to safety.

5 UNEXPECTED CALAMITIES

Once common birds in sudden danger.

Lesser Flamingo

What kind of buffer does a species need to render its extinction all but impossible? The intuitive answer would be a very high population spread over a wide area. The higher a bird's population, so the logic dictates, the least likelihood that it will disappear off the face of the earth.

Sometimes this is not enough. The clearest refutation concerns the infamous demise of the Passenger Pigeon (*Ectopistes migratorius*) in the USA at the end of the 19th century. This case is so astonishing that it bears repeating again and again. This bird was, if the contemporary descriptions are taken at face value, perhaps the most abundant species that the world has ever seen. There have been estimates of a total population of 3-5 billion individuals at the time of European settlement. The average breeding colony covered 16km by 5km of forest, and flocks would fill the skies for days on end. Yet by the end of the 19th century the species was doomed; the last wild record was in 1900 and the last captive bird died in 1914. The reasons for the extinction included shooting, deforestation, disease and a biological need to exist in large numbers. Once the species sunk below a certain threshold of abundance, its fate was sealed.

While this is not the place for a detailed treatise on the Passenger Pigeon, its story shouts loud that a large population is never enough to keep a bird safe. And while we shouldn't get carried away about every species in the world staring over the precipice, we should at least be mindful that any decline needs investigation and that no species should be taken for granted.

The species in this chapter were once too common to worry about. Now, however, alarm bells are ringing. Let's hope that, in these cases, help doesn't come too late.

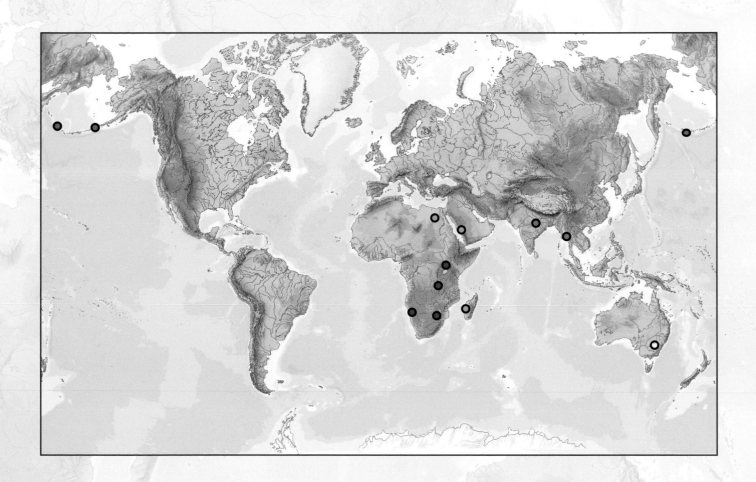

WHITE-RUMPED VULTURE

Gyps bengalensis

The death of the undertakers

The story of the White-rumped Vulture is a model illustration of how the population of a once common bird can suddenly crash towards near-extinction without warning. In the late 1980s, this particular species was just about the last bird you would expect ever to get into trouble. It was extremely abundant on the Indian Subcontinent and north towards Nepal and west towards Pakistan, with a population counted in the millions; indeed, it was thought to be the most numerous bird of prey in the world. It was a familiar sight to anyone living in or visiting the towns and villages of northern India,

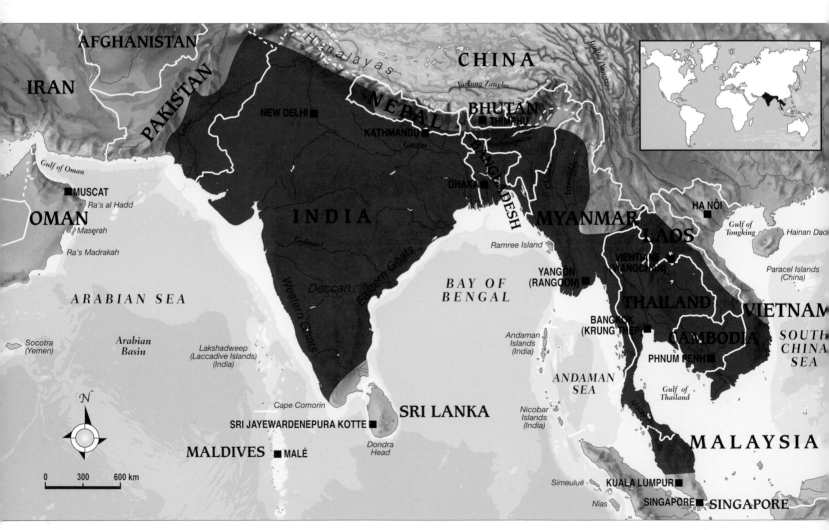

Left: In common with other vultures, the White-rumped has enormous broad wings, an adaptation for extending periods of soaring and searching.

Below: White-rumped Vultures were once a familiar sight in the cities of southern Asia.

where colonies of these birds would live on the outskirts, each day clearing up the local animal carcasses with healthy efficiency. There was no persecution and no malevolence towards the birds. In fact, they enjoyed widespread tolerance – indeed benevolence – from the human population, who were aware of their ability to clear up waste. The White-rumped Vulture was doing about as well as any bird anywhere.

Then, in the mid-1990s, people began to notice that there weren't so many vultures around anymore. The first indications came from the world-famous Keoladeo Ghana National Park (also known as Bharatpur) south of Delhi, where in the 1987-88 breeding season there were 353 nests of vultures in the tall trees and the species was abundant. By 1996-97 there were suddenly less than half the number of nests, only about 150, a worrying drop by any standards. The decline continued until there were a pitiful 20 nests in 1998-99 and, by 2003, the vulture was extinct at this site.

This alarming decline began to be mirrored elsewhere, as teams from the Bombay Natural History Society investigated other parts of India. The toll at Bharatpur, it seemed, was the tip of an iceberg, and a decline of vultures of disastrous proportions had been visited on the lands of south Asia. Together with declines noted in nearby Pakistan and Nepal, it is estimated that numbers of vultures across the region had dropped by an eye-popping 99.9 per cent in the 15 years from 1993 to 2007. Tens of millions of birds are thought to have died. Almost unbelievably, the White-rumped Vulture, with a population now down below the 10,000 mark, and possibly as low as 2,500,

was now in grave danger of extinction, along with several other species of Asian vultures, including the Indian Vulture (*Gyps indicus*) and the Slender-billed Vulture (*Gyps tenuirostris*).

At first the cause was thought to be some kind of infectious disease limited to vultures. Then researchers from the Peregrine Fund in Pakistan, testing tissue samples from the dead birds, discovered

WHITE-RUMPED VULTURE
Gyps bengalensis

that the real cause was an anti-inflammatory drug which was used to treat injured cattle, Diclofenac. When the cattle that had been treated died, the vultures would ingest the drug and it would kill them from renal failure. Birds that were affected died a slow and painful death.

The problem was that Diclofenac was widely and routinely used across the whole of south Asia. In some parts of the world the problem would not have been so great, since cow carcasses would have been removed from the system. However, to adherents of Hinduism it is, of course, taboo to consume cow flesh, and once dead the carcasses are typically left in place, to be removed by the birds. To make matters worse, the researchers found that if only 1 per cent of all carcasses in a region contained traces of Diclofenac, this was enough to cause the catastrophic die-off of the vultures. The scene had been set for this environmental disaster.

To the credit of all agencies involved, Diclofenac was quickly banned in Nepal and India as soon as its effect on vultures was understood. This decision was doubtless helped by the facts that the feral dog population spiralled upward along with the incidence of rabies in humans, and that an alternative, albeit more expensive, anti-inflammatory drug called Meloxicam was available and proved harmless to the birds. Now, of course, the practice will have to follow from the knowledge. It is a long and tedious business to replace one drug with another, and Diclofenac is still widely used in Asia, despite the ban. However, great efforts are being made to educate people about the effects of Diclofenac, and also to teach them about the vital role vultures play in environmental and

public health. Eventually, it is hoped that Diclofenac will disappear.

In the meantime, other threats to the vultures have taken hold. Since they are no longer common, disturbance at the colonies can now be a problem, and in South-East Asia there have been population decreases of White-rumped Vultures pre-dating the Diclofenac episode, mainly owing to agricultural intensification and a reduced population of large wild animals upon which the birds feed.

On the plus side, it is highly fortunate that the cause of the slump was discovered before the birds actually became extinct: another couple of years and it would have probably been too late. It might still be too late, but at least there is still some hope. There is already an intensive captive-breeding programme underway, managed by the Bombay Natural History Society and the UK's Royal Society for the Protection of Birds. In 2007 the first White-rumped Vulture chicks were hatched in aviaries in Haryana in India.

A splendidly innovative remedial project that has also been tried is the concept of the 'Vulture Restaurant', an open area where poison-free carcasses can be provided specially for the birds, and the number of visitors monitored by the locals. So long as the birds can be consistently attracted to these areas, away from potential contamination, this could prove to be an excellent way of keeping the population stable until diclofenac is finally removed from the system. The restaurants are currently operating well in Nepal and also Cambodia, where their populations are less affected by the drug and it is a previous lack of food that has contributed to the population decline.

It would be hard to overestimate the impact on the

Indian Subcontinent were the vultures to disappear completely. They are a vitally important component of the natural cleaning up of ecosystems; they are immune even to putrid flesh, and will eat the most revolting of carcasses with ill-concealed relish. Without them, there has already been a sharp and worrying rise in the number of rats and feral dogs in India, which has resulted, in the latter case, in a higher incidence of rabies.

Of course, vultures are also culturally significant in India. Apart from their well-known place in rural village life across the majority Hindu population, they are exceptionally important for some religious minorities. For example, the Parsi religion, a form of Zoroastrianism, prohibits the cremation or interment of the dead. Instead, corpses are placed up on so-called 'Towers of Silence' to be disposed of naturally – typically by vultures. These sky-burials are now being hampered by the lack of vultures; where bodies were

Above: A vulture scrum such as this is now a very rare sight anywhere in Asia. The populations of three species of these scavenging birds have collapsed.

once stripped to bones in a few hours, they are now remaining in situ for many days, and numbers are piling up. It is a very practical and agonising problem for Parsis, as well as being a public health issue.

It is easy to imagine how the practice of sky-burials might have entered the traditions of the Parsis and become an accepted practice. For the scavenging vultures have always been part of the currency of everyday life and death in India and elsewhere, and their sheer abundance would have suggested to people that they, like other parts of society's fabric, would always be there. Yet in the last few years the unthinkable has truly happened: an India without vultures is not just a serious possibility, but already a reality in many places.

SOOTY FALCON
Falco concolor

The migrant killers

There's not much ordinary about the Sooty Falcon. It occurs in extreme habitats, has highly unusual breeding behaviour and an almost unique migratory pathway. Even the apparently unremarkable coloration works smartly and sleekly upon the bird itself.

Only in recent months has the Sooty Falcon become a candidate for this book. It is one of those species that, for many years, has been considered no more than a rare and localized oddity. The latest counts, however, have plunged the species on to the Near Threatened list, and things in reality could be much worse than that.

The Sooty Falcon is a bird that breeds in the hot, arid, treeless landscapes in North Africa and the Middle East. It is one of the few species that occurs in the inland parts of Arabia and the Sahara Desert, on cliffs and rocky outcrops that don't see much life. The same sort of extremes are found on coastal cliffs and islands in the Red Sea and the Gulf, and here too Sooty Falcons hunt for birds passing by, and pick up large insects, bats and the occasional rodent. Many

Left: The sleek Sooty Falcon is an arid-zone species showing a number of peculiar behavioural adapatations.

pairs are found in very isolated and remote situations. The local climate can be so hot that it is only possible for the hunters to be active at dawn and dusk.

For most of the year, breeding in such places would be almost impossible – the biomass of potential food items would be simply too low to sustain bringing up a brood of youngsters, regardless of the skill of the adult birds. But for a couple of months in the autumn, this situation turns around completely. Flyways that, for the summer months, held no passing traffic suddenly become crowded with streams of migrating birds heading south after breeding in Europe and Asia. The travellers provide the Sooty Falcons with a glut of food and, with meat readily available, now is the time that they breed. They lay their eggs in July and August, and the chicks hatch in time for the peak movement of passing birds.

Sooty Falcons don't seem to have a specialized feeding technique. They catch most of their prey with a rapid approach from just above or, less often, perform fast dives from a considerable height. Studies suggest that the greatest toll may not be on the smallest prey, but on larger species such as shrikes and bee-eaters. Indeed, the latter seem to be particularly important. Nevertheless, it is doubtless the sheer quantity of available prey that makes the late breeding so expedient

After their late nesting, Sooty Falcons embark on a migration that brings them, bizarrely, all the way to the offshore Indian Ocean island of Madagascar, 1,000km from the African continent. Only one other Eurasian landbird, the ecologically closely similar Eleonora's Falcon (*Falco eleonorae*), follows a similar route to the same destination. On arrival Sooty

SOOTY FALCON
Falco concolor

Falcons change their habits completely. They eschew extreme habitats in favour of much more conventional ones, such as woodland edge, lakes and rivers, paddyfields and even towns, where they can be seen easily. They also undergo a change of diet, shifting to snatching large insects in flight, creatures such as ants, termites and locusts. And rather than taking their captured prey to a perch for dismembering, Sooty Falcons can eat insects on the hop, transferring them from talons to bill in mid-air and allowing themselves to tuck in when food is plentiful. They often gather in groups to feed on swarming insects in the evening, sometimes in company with Eleonora's Falcons.

The exact route taken by Sooty Falcons between the Middle East and Madagascar used to be something of a mystery, until in 2008 a single bird from Abu Dhabi in the UAE was fitted with a transmitter and tracked by satellite on its outward migration. It left its breeding grounds in October, and was followed down through Saudi Arabia to Ethiopia, Kenya, Tanzania and Mozambique before making the crossing over to Madagascar. By the end of its journey it had covered a total of 6,700km. Nobody knows why it continues on from the African mainland to Madagascar, but it might be to avoid competition with other Eurasian falcons that are insectivorous on their wintering grounds.

Until recently the Sooty Falcon was considered to be under no threat at all. It has a very large distribution, and so many breeding pairs are found in isolated and inaccessible parts of the Palearctic arid zone that it was thought that they would remain safe where they were. However, observations in the wintering areas in the last few years have revealed a

Opposite: Sandy desert cliffs in north-east Africa or Arabia are typical breeding habitat for the Sooty Falcon, in sharp contrast to its winter quarters.

Left and below: The Sooty Falcon's breeding areas include some of the world's most inhospitable, lifeless terrain. The predators time their breeding to coincide with the autumn southbound rush of small migratory birds.

significant drop in numbers, and also unveiled a better idea of the true population. It was once thought that the population numbered in the tens of thousands, but nowadays just a few thousand at most have been seen south of the Equator in winter. Furthermore, a recent estimate from Saudi Arabia put the breeding population there at 500 pairs; and since this is considered to be the bird's heartland, there may be no more than double this in any given year.

The Sooty Falcon has long been known as a very difficult bird to census, and it could well be that the current concerns are overcooked. On the other hand, the bird could just as easily be in serious trouble. It is one of those species that is hard to pin down.

What will be needed in future is careful protection and monitoring of the known and accessible breeding areas, such as those in the Gulf close to major conurbations. These populations have steadily declined in numbers over the last few years, for reasons that are not yet clear. Perhaps the problem is a decline in food availability in Madagascar, or on the journey. Or perhaps there are smaller streams of migratory birds moving south in autumn. If it were the latter, that would have serious implications in the conservation world, well beyond the concerns for the fate of the Sooty Falcon.

REGENT HONEYEATER
Xanthomyza phrygia

currently estimated that the surviving population numbers somewhere between 500 and 1,500 individuals, and it is continuing to drop. Birds are regularly seen in only four widely scattered locations.

So what is it that has made the Regent Honeyeater such a threatened species – so much more so than other members of its family? What sets it apart from other moderately widespread Australian birds?

The answer is far from completely understood, although a great deal about the Regent Honeyeater's ecology has now been unveiled. It occurs mainly in forests on the inland slopes of the Great Dividing Range, where the dominant trees are certain species of ironbarks and box, both of which are types of narrow-leaved eucalyptus, the trees that dominate much of Australia. The honeyeater seems to be particularly drawn to the moister sections of such forests or savannas where creeks and streams flow, and one of its primary requirements for breeding is a large and very reliable source of nectar. It feeds almost exclusively in the upper canopy of its favoured trees, supping from the flowers, but also taking insects and, frequently, such extras as honeydew and manna (sugary exudates from animals and plants). It is often sociable, and sometimes nests in colonies, or at least aggregations of pairs. The Regent Honeyeater is a conspicuous, big and aggressive bird, fighting its corner against members of its own species and the many other honeyeaters that are after the same nectar.

One of the Regent Honeyeater's clear problems is a loss of habitat. Its favoured rich forests have always been on the most fertile parts of the lowlands, those most suitable for agriculture, so now it is estimated that about 75 per cent of its potential habitat has been lost to farming. This honeyeater also suffers badly from habitat degradation, a much more subtle threat than the removal of forest. So, for example, where the biggest and tallest trees of its favourite forests are removed and do not regenerate, the Regent Honeyeater cannot cope. It is also suspected that the opening out of habitats has benefited some of this bird's competitors, fellow honeyeaters such as miners (*Manorina*) and friarbirds (*Philemon*), which feed in similar places. All of these factors, together with the bird's wandering lifestyle, seem to have conspired to cause its disappearance.

At present, conservationists in Australia have been working hard to protect and maintain the Regent Honeyeater's remaining wild habitats and, at the same time, a captive-breeding programme is reaping rewards: 27 captive-bred birds were released in Chiltern National Park, Victoria, in 2008 to augment the population already there. It should be possible to arrest the Regent Honeyeater's slide towards extinction.

Nevertheless, there is something deeply disturbing about this particular case of a bird becoming endangered. It is the Regent Honeyeater's evident ordinariness that is worrying: not an island freak, not so fussy that it seems impossible to please, not with a restricted geographical spread, not supposedly much different from any number of other species, honeyeaters or otherwise. One might suggest that, if the Regent Honeyeater can get into trouble, any number of other Australian birds can.

That gloomy prospect suggests that, back in the 1940s, the choice of which species was likely to become the rarest was a lot wider than anyone could have imagined.

Below: Very much a bird of rich, moist forest, particularly dominated by eucalypts called ironbark and box, the Regent Honeyeater suffers even from subtle modifications of its habitat.

RED-LEGGED KITTIWAKE

Rissa brevirostris

A global warning?

Not so long ago, there was no way that a bird such as the Red-legged Kittiwake could have featured in a book such as this. However, its inclusion is a story of our times. Once thought to be inviolate in its Arctic breeding grounds and oceanic wintering areas, even a bird such as this is now known to be vulnerable to over-fishing and the unpredictable hazards of climate change.

Many birdwatchers know its relative the Black-legged Kittiwake (*R. tridactyla*) well enough, since it is a fairly common breeding species both in Europe,

north Asia and North America. Those who have heard of the Red-legged Kittiwake would consider it something of an exotic bird, one that could only be seen on a far-flung and expensive birding visit to its breeding cliffs in the Bering Sea. It has an extremely restricted distribution on just four main groups of islands: the Pribilof Islands, where most of the population occurs; and three sets of Aleutian Islands: the Commander Islands, Buldir Island and Bugoslof Island. On these islands the bird can seen numerous enough – there are 123,000 birds on St George in the

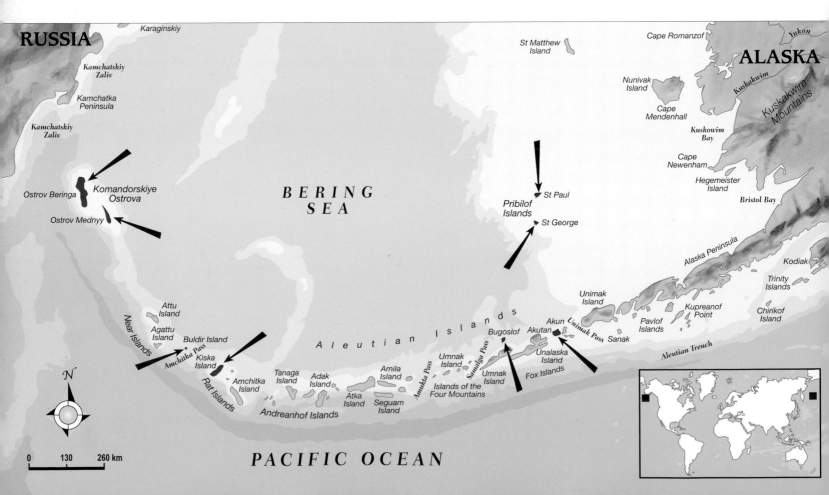

Left: A Red-legged Kittiwake shows off its most obvious characteristic. Its commoner black-legged relative has longer legs and is paler grey on the back.

Below: Red-legged Kittiwakes spend most of their lives flying over deep water. They feed mainly at night, when their favoured foods of fish and squid commute closer to the surface of the sea.

Pribilofs, for example. But anywhere else the Red-legged kittiwake is virtually impossible to find.

One of the interesting puzzles about the Red-legged Kittiwake is what makes it different from its much commoner relative? How can there be two species of kittiwake in the Bering Sea, and not just one? One intriguing difference is that the Red-legged Kittiwake has a larger eye than the Black-legged, and this may be related to the fact that it feeds more during the night, when certain fish and squid species habitually come to the surface under cover of darkness. Certainly, several of its most important foods in the breeding season, including Lampfish (*Stenobrachius leucopsarus*), move upwards at night and the Red-legged Kittiwake, which has a shorter bill than its relative, can easily dip down in flight to catch them. If it is mainly a night feeder, this would make it differ from Black-legged Kittiwake.

It seems that another subtle distinction from its commoner relative is that it travels further away from its colony each time when feeding young. It is thought that most adult birds make regular foraging trips to the edge of the continental shelf, in waters up to 2,000m deep, where they specialize on just a handful of species of foods: the Lampfish and squids mentioned above, plus the Walleye Pollock (*Theragra chalcogramma*). At times the birds may be away from the nest for 12 hours and, as a result, their young take slightly longer than equivalent Black-legged Kittiwakes to reach maturity. The adults also typically only lay a single egg rather than two, as in the case of the Black-legged Kittiwake.

Nevertheless, these distinctions are subtle. Red-legged and Black-legged Kittiwakes are often found in

RED-LEGGED KITTIWAKE
Rissa brevirostris

the same flocks in the Bering Sea, feeding over the same shoals of fish, and they even share the same breeding cliffs – although the Red-legged Kittiwakes traditionally build on narrower cliff ledges (less than 14cm wide) than Black-legged Kittiwakes. The nests of both species are remarkable, just platforms of mud or plants attached to extraordinarily vertiginous cliffs above foaming seas. In contrast to most chicks of gull species, which roam around the parents' small territory, kittiwake chicks sit tight in the nest, and with good reason; one false move could mean disaster.

Once breeding is over, both adults and young fly out and into the ocean, where they effectively disappear from the sight of people. The birds do not linger by their breeding islands and there are very few records in the winter. Some go to the pack ice, others travel into the Gulf of Alaska, but most of them disperse over the deepest waters, a habitat far removed from land.

It seems hard to grasp that a bird with such a peripheral relationship with people should somehow be threatened by us, especially in the remotest reaches of its subarctic range. Yet even here humans come, bringing their commercial pressures. No less than half of all the sea fish consumed in the USA come from the Bering Sea region, and in 2002, 1.53 million tonnes of pollock were caught in Alaska waters alone, constituting perhaps a billion individual fish. Despite the apparent loneliness and isolation, several thousand vessels ply the waters that the kittiwakes also use as their hunting ground. It is an uneven contest.

Not surprisingly, the pollock population crashed in the early 1990s in the zones beyond the 200-mile limits of Russia and Alaska. Indeed, almost all the fisheries have seen declines of various sorts, and it is clear that, between them, the trawlers are catching too many fish. However, the distribution of these northern fish species, and the direct effects of commercial trawling, are still poorly understood.

Meanwhile, the Red-legged Kittiwake has undoubtedly declined. Between the 1970s and the 1990s the Red-legged Kittiwake colony at St George on the Pribilof Islands fell in numbers by 44 per cent, and the nearby smaller colony on St Paul also became depleted. Admittedly some colonies elsewhere have seen an increase, but the Pribilof colonies contain 70 per cent of the breeding birds, and the overall drop amounts to about a third. This means that the Red-legged Kittiwake is currently listed as Vulnerable.

Of course, the world is now waking up to the all-pervading threat of climate change. The world is guaranteed to warm up, and all kinds of predictions have been made for what will happen as a result. Ocean currents are among the hardest to surmise, but already, in various parts of the world, alterations in currents have resulted in local failure of breeding seabird populations, caused by their fish supplies going elsewhere. And this possibility would be particularly destructive for the Red-legged Kittiwake. This species already has to commute 120–150km away from its breeding cliffs to obtain food for the young. If the distribution of its favoured food were to alter, and move the best fishing areas still further away, it might not be possible for the adults to bring up their young – the commuting trip would simply be too long. If that happened and the situation persisted, that could tip the relatively numerous Red-legged Kittiwake towards extinction.

Below: A Red-legged Kittiwake at the site of its incomplete nest. This species breeds on extremely narrow cliff ledges, usually less than 14cm wide.

LESSER FLAMINGO

Phoeniconaias minor

Abundance threatened

Yes, this is the proverbial flamingo of the African Rift Valley lakes, the one that crowds in its millions and turns the water pink from the air. This is the species that you have admired on television, as you followed the chicks from their strange mud castles, via treacherous walks across dried-out lake-beds to the elegance and mass sociability of adulthood. This is the flamingo that defines the exotic and brings visitors to warm countries. It is the iconic and most flamingo-ish of flamingos: pink and abundant and African.

So what is it doing in a book about threatened birds?

Well, the answer is that there is always peril in specialization. And there are few more specialized birds in the world than flamingos.

Look at the bill, for a start. It is a bill like no other, a bill that has to be used upside-down. It is uneven, with a small upper mandible and a large, deep-keeled lower mandible, and it is also characteristically kinked in the middle. The kink is extremely important because it allows the flamingo to open its bill to a consistent width, rather than the tip opening far wider than the base, as it would if it were straight. The upper mandible, with its V-shaped roof, fits tightly into a groove in the lower mandible, so tightly that

Opposite: The Lesser Flamingo's long, spindly legs allow it to wade in very deep water. It is perfectly capable of swimming, too.

Left: Flamingo lakes look attractive, but they are often severely alkaline or saline, located in oppressively hot places and generally inhospitable to life.

there seems no discernible gap between them. On the surfaces of both interlocking mandibles is a network of minute comb-like structures, called lamellae, which lie 120 micrometres apart and actually form a net when the mandibles are shut to catch tiny organisms in suspension as they flow past. Meanwhile the tongue, which fits in a groove within the lower mandible, works like a piston, pumping water in and out up to 17 times a second and trapping the organisms on which the flamingo feeds.

Not surprisingly, the Lesser Flamingo has an unusual diet to go with its extraordinary bill. It relies almost exclusively on microscopic blue-green algae (especially *Spirulina platensis*) and diatoms. These are too small to be of much nutritional value to other birds, just 40–200 micrometres across, and so the flamingo is able virtually to monopolize the habitat – hence its occurrence in thousands and millions on suitable lakes.

While it is convenient to avoid competition with other birds, the habitat of the Lesser Flamingo is nonetheless exceptionally harsh at times. The flamingo only occurs on very alkaline or saline lakes, and cannot survive for long in fresh water. Such lakes

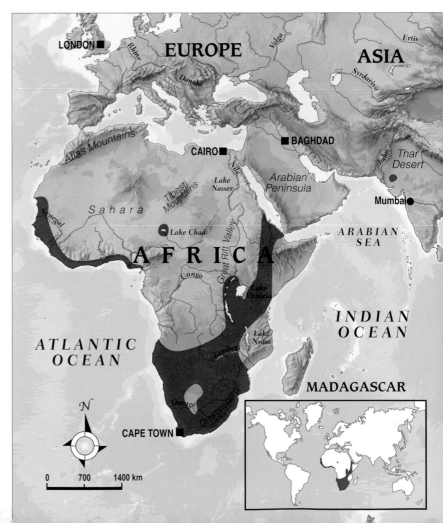

LESSER FLAMINGO
Phoeniconaias minor

are so inhospitable that they keep the Lesser Flamingos safe, as well as fed. No ground predator risks trying to walk through the sticky, corrosive mud, which at some of the birds' breeding areas can be at a temperature of 55–56°C.

Lesser Flamingos are among the most sociable of all birds. In the past they used to be found in millions, both at breeding and loafing areas (at Lake Magadi in 1962, for example, there was a colony of 1,200,000 pairs). This ensures that they do many things communally, even courtship displays. It is possible, for instance, to see thousands of birds all at once holding their heads up and waving them from side to side. Nest-building and other breeding behaviour can also be highly synchronized, especially within subdivisions of the colony, with all the nests being finished at roughly the same time – a colony of 500,000 pairs may shift 15,000 tonnes of mud for building their cones. All the young may hatch within a few days of each other, and leave the nest at similar times – in some colonies the youngsters have to march from the mudflats to permanent lagoons up to 30km away. They then may gather into enormous crèches, sometimes 300,000 strong, guarded by just a few adults. The young members of these crèches have a unique predator-deterrent strategy, in which they bunch even closer together and bury their heads in each other's plumage. And somehow, when the coast is clear, despite the melee, their parents have to find their own young and deliver food.

The extreme habitat and extremes of behaviour of the Lesser Flamingo have a serious downside. There are very few places in the world capable of supporting even medium-sized colonies. So, for example, the entire East African population currently breeds on only one lake, Lake Natron in Tanzania (with 75 per cent of the world population), while the main southern African populations are on the Etosha Pan in Namibia, the West African birds in Mauritania and the Asian birds in the Rann of Kutch in north-west India. Although the birds occupy a network of sites outside the breeding season and, to a lesser extent, for breeding, the destruction or modification of just a few key sites could set the population into freefall.

A good recent example is the case of Lake Natron. In 2007 the Tanzanian government and Tata Chemicals put forward a plan to develop a large soda ash extraction and processing plant on the shores of the lake. The idea was that the plant would produce 500,000 tonnes of sodium carbonate a year by pumping 530 cubic metres of brine through its system every hour, and pipes would be laid in a network across the site. Besides its effect on the lake itself, the development put forward a plan to build a large block of accommodation for more than a thousand workers, plus road and rail links. Although the plan is still subject to an official environmental impact assessment, it is hard to see how its effect on the water levels and general disturbance could have anything but a significant impact on the flamingos. Not surprisingly, all the conservation agencies are against such a potentially damaging development.

For the moment the plan has been put on hold, but the message it sends is clear. No breeding site for the highly specialized Lesser Flamingo is safe and, therefore, even this very locally superabundant species is not protected by the sheer size of its numbers.

Left: Flamingos are among the most sociable of all birds. They indulge in many communal displays, including waving their heads from side to side.

Below: The incomparable sight of flamingos in flight. Almost everywhere they occur in numbers, Lesser Flamingos are a tourist attraction – and this could be their saving grace.

6 LOST CAUSES?

Optimism fades – or has gone completely.

Philippine Eagle

There are about 200 species of birds currently recognized as Critically Endangered in the world, with officially a 50 per cent chance of extinction within the next 10 years (or three generations of the species). The fates of all of them hang in the balance but, as has happened through the centuries, some will inevitably fare better than others in the future owing to circumstances such as protection, discoveries of new populations or, conversely, disasters and the continuing destruction of habitat.

Which, though, will be the first to fall over the precipice of extinction? It is anybody's guess, of course, but guesses have their uses, and in this section I am highlighting five species whose future seems to be particularly worrying, for a variety of reasons. Or actually, there are four that are worrying; it seems almost certain that one is lost to extinction already. Another, incidentally, is not even listed as Critically Endangered yet.

Why make such a selection? Well, firstly it is to highlight these birds' plight, away from any unjustifiable optimism. Secondly, it is to balance other chapters which give tales of rediscovery and astonishing recovery. It would be wrong for any reader to come away from this book satisfied that enough work is being done around the globe to protect everything, because that simply is not the case. For sure, there are many heart-warming efforts around the world being made to stop species becoming extinct, but it seems inevitable that these stories will soon become the exception. Instead we will probably begin to hear, increasingly, that fights for survival are being lost.

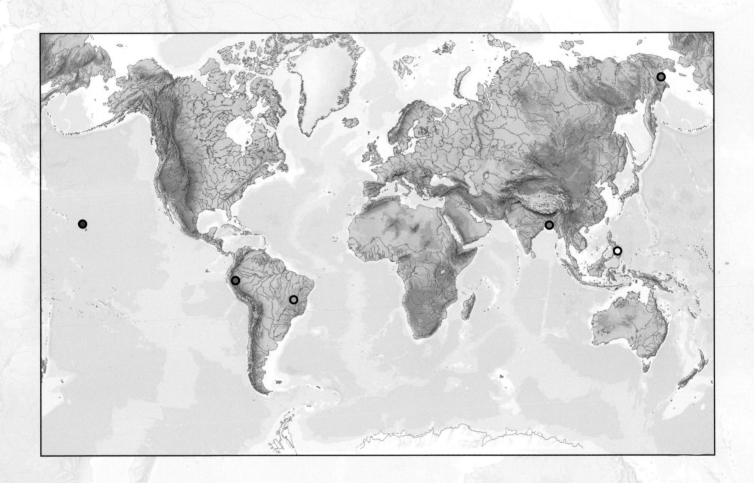

SPOON-BILLED SANDPIPER

Eurynorhynchus pygmeus

A wanderer without a refuge

There are some endangered species around the world that just look doomed, and at present it is very difficult to feel optimistic about the future of the Spoon-billed Sandpiper. Only in the last few years upgraded from Vulnerable to Critically Endangered, this highly distinctive wader has suffered a series of heavy blows from all sides. A number of them were even known to have been killed in the Asian tsunami of 2004.

The Spoon-billed Sandpiper is a real gem. About the size of a Little Stint (*Calidris minuta*) or a 'peep' sandpiper, it is instantly distinguished by its unique spatulate bill, a feature that isn't shared by any other wader, and by hardly any other bird in the world. Although the bill is often swept from side to side in shallow water in the manner of a spoonbill (*Platalea* spp.), quite what the function of the bill is, and what competitive advantage it might confer on its owner, simply isn't yet understood. In mud the Spoon-billed Sandpiper often simply picks from the surface in common with other waders, although it can appear at times as though the bill is 'glued' to the surface as the bird wanders back and forth without lifting its head.

This charismatic species is restricted as a breeding bird to one very small area of north-eastern Russia, along the coast from the Chukotsk Peninsula down towards the Kamchatka Peninsula. It was probably always historically limited to this area, and was never common. Within its range it seems to have highly specialized habitat requirements, apparently only using lagoon spits with sparse, tundra vegetation (crowberry/lichen or dwarf birch/willow/sedge), and these always adjacent to muddy estuaries. All sites recorded except one have been within 5km of the sea.

Once the Spoon-billed Sandpiper has chosen its nesting area it is extremely faithful to it; 65 per cent of all breeding birds return to exactly the same site each year. It is also, most unusually for a small shorebird, faithful to its mate throughout the season and from one season to another (many small shorebirds are highly promiscuous). Incubation is shared and, once the eggs hatch, both sexes may tend the chicks (which have spoon-shaped bills from the start and can sweep

them in the same style as the adults), at least for the first few days. Then the female leaves the breeding grounds and the male attends to the youngsters until they are about 20 days old.

After breeding, Spoon-billed Sandpipers make a long migration southwards to winter on muddy

Above: The precise function of the Spoon-billed Sandpiper's bill still isn't understood. When feeding, the bird sweeps its head from side to side in the manner of an avocet (*Recurvirostra* spp.) or spoonbill (*Platalea* spp.).

BRAZILIAN MERGANSER

Mergus octosetaceus

A fast-disappearing inhabitant of rushing rivers and streams

This is one of those species which, until recently, was tipping towards extinction without a great deal of fanfare. In many ways it could represent any number of species of birds found in small parts of large continents: poorly known, rarely seen and attractive without being especially spectacular, species that could surreptitiously be reaching critical levels without being noticed very much. Admittedly, the situation with the Brazilian Merganser has now improved, with an action plan drawn up, regular surveys of its population undertaken and its status meriting a BirdLife International listing as Critically Endangered, with all the attention which that guarantees. Yet it is still possible that this interesting bird may become extinct in the next 20 years.

It is probable that the merganser was always rare. Historically, it has only ever been recorded in three countries: Paraguay, Argentina and Brazil. It is now almost certainly extinct in Paraguay and Argentina, while in Brazil there remain two or three so-called 'strongholds' for the species, although they hardly qualify as such, with a modest maximum of 81 birds at the top site, Serra da Canastra National Park, Minas Gerais (2002). Everywhere it has declined sharply.

Part of the Brazilian Merganser's rarity can be attributed to its unusual and restricted habitat. It is only found along clear, fast-flowing, shallow rivers, where it dives for fish, snails and insect larvae among rapids, waterfalls and deeper pools. It copes with turbulent water, even waterfalls, with ease, and it is much more agile on dry land than most diving ducks. Suitable habitat tends to occur on the upper reaches of rivers between 200 and 1,400m, and it seems that rather small tributaries can suffice. Suitable rivers may flow through forest or grassland, but it seems to be essential for the merganser's welfare that they are as undisturbed as possible.

In common with many ducks that breed along rivers, the Brazilian Merganser is fiercely territorial. A

pair seems to require at least 8km of river to itself, with some holding court along 14km; the difference seems to have something to do with the precise nature of the habitat, with such attributes as water speed, fish density, number of rapids and condition of riparian vegetation seeming to be important. Birds

Above: A dark grey-brown base colour to its plumage means that the Brazilian Merganser is well camouflaged against the rocks upon which it often stands.

BRAZILIAN MERGANSER
Mergus octosetaceus

don't tolerate intrusions, and fights between pairs have regularly been recorded. However, not surprisingly, this low density means that the carrying capacity in a given location is necessarily restricted, keeping the population low.

Brazilian Mergansers breed in holes in trees, or among rocks. One of the first sites to be discovered was 25m above the ground in a tree-hole, which is always an incongruous-looking site for a duck. Pairs are as fiercely loyal to one another as they are to their territory, and remain in each other's company throughout the year. Both male and female contribute significantly to the care of the young (in many duck species this is not the case). When all is settled they can be highly productive; in the Serra da Canastra National Park, four monitored breeding pairs managed to bring up a total of 70 young in only five years.

The Brazilian Merganser is a very difficult bird to observe. It feeds mainly in the morning and evening, and seems to spend a great deal of time just sitting

still on rocks, logs or branches of emergent vegetation, in the shade or out of sight. Its dark plumage makes it difficult to see against the water, and the nature of the turbulent riverine habitat means that, even when the birds are actively feeding, they are still hard to pick up. Furthermore, with so few birds along a given stretch of river, finding a Brazilian Merganser can be quite a challenge.

There is no doubt, however, that this species has declined enormously in recent years. There was once a population in Argentina but extensive surveys have located just one bird since 1992, and it is probably now extinct there. Further problems have occurred along river systems in Brazil. The main threat is from damming for hydroelectric power schemes, which is known already to have caused catastrophic losses in merganser numbers wherever it has taken place. Another problem is deforestation, which increases turbidity in the rivers where the merganser occurs, and the concomitant agricultural intensification along tracts of river additionally causes pollution. There have also been occasional problems with tourist activities such as white-water rafting. These can

Opposite: Easily overlooked, the Brazilian Merganser was not considered to be seriously threatened until recently.

Above left: Many diving ducks take a quick look before a dive to check where any fish might be, a practice sometimes known as 'snorkelling'.

Above: Brazilian Mergansers occur on and beside fast-flowing streams in the hills. The birds with white throats in this image are youngsters.

disturb the birds and modify the river system in adverse ways, such as increasing water turbidity and modifying the riverbank. It is astonishing that some of this has taken place inside national parks.

All in all, the sensitive Brazilian Merganser faces a high number of threats to its existence. Space and peace are not easily found in the modern world, and this is one species that suffers with their passing. The wild populations are in serious trouble, and a captive breeding effort is not yet underway. There are already fewer than 250 birds left, and it seems highly possible that further declines will occur. A serious disaster at the stronghold of Serra da Canastra, such as pollution, could push this species to the brink.

PHILIPPINE EAGLE

Pithecophaga jefferyi

Running out of space

It will hardly be news to anybody reading this book that deforestation is a serious global issue threatening the world's wildlife. Everybody knows that forests are being cut down at a frightening rate, and that the animals that depend on them are disappearing too. However, as yet there have been few proven major cases of death by deforestation: large animals that have been driven to extinction by the cutting down of trees. Many are known to be severely endangered, of course, such as orang-utans (*Pongo* spp.) or Javan Rhinoceros (*Rhinoceros sondaicus*), but these are all somehow managing to hold on. Unfortunately, however, the giant eagle of the Philippine Islands could well be one of the first big flagship species to succumb if things remain as they are.

The Philippine Eagle is a real giant, a top-level predator with a 2m wingspan; it is one of the three

Opposite: Even though it is a huge raptor, the nature of its habits and habitat, not to mention its rarity, means that it can be very difficult to catch a glimpse of a Philippine Eagle.

Left: The eagle's bill is the ideal tool for tearing apart the arboreal mammals that make up its diet.

largest eagles in the world. In days gone by the Philippine Eagle used to be known as the Monkey-eating Eagle, and there were occasional rumours of human beings disappearing mysteriously in the Philippine forests. But, while this sort of nonsense adds a little extra drama to the eagle's reputation, the truth is still impressive. The Philippine Eagle takes almost any medium-sized animal of the forest, including the occasional monkey, but its favourite foods are actually of two main kinds: the Asian Palm Civet (*Paradoxurus hermaphroditus*) and the Philippine Flying Lemur (*Cynocephalus volans*). The latter is a strange, vaguely squirrel-like mammal that has a flap between its limbs and can glide from tree to tree. In some studies these creatures have been known to constitute 90 per cent of the Philippine Eagle's diet.

Despite its size, the Philippine Eagle can be an extremely difficult bird to see in the wild. It generally remains just above or within the forest canopy when on the lookout for food, and will often simply sit quietly on a perch waiting for prey to come into view. When the need arises, it has the long wings and tail of

●●●●●●●●●○○○○ **PHILIPPINE EAGLE**
Pithecophaga jefferyi

a highly manoeuvrable hunter, and large talons to make a rapid kill. For its nest it selects a huge forest tree crown, which can be 30m above ground, and builds a stick platform that can be 1.5m across. But despite this apparent grandeur, the nest can still be very difficult to find in dense forest. In short, the Philippine Eagle is a deep forest specialist, occurring only in pristine tracts dominated by tall dipterocarps.

As befitting a predator at the top of the food chain, the Philippine Eagle would never have been numerous, but it was certainly once far more widespread on the larger islands of the Philippine archipelago than it is now. Deforestation there has been rife for decades, and even now much of what is left has been leased to logging concessions. There is no doubt that the eagle must have declined severely since its discovery in 1896, both in numbers and range, but it is unknown by how much, and this has hampered the conservation efforts. Indeed, in the 1970s some gloomy counts declared that there were no more than about 50 birds, and it was judged already to be on the verge of extinction. That proved to be erroneous and more recent estimates are in the hundreds, with perhaps 500 birds in the wild altogether. But this is an extraordinary difficult bird to census: highly secretive, and found in dense and often inhospitable habitat, and the figure has only been reached by extrapolation of breeding densities on Mindanao, where most birds remain.

Even if 500 birds sounds like a good number, a whole set of worrying statistics indicates that, within a few years, the population could crash to unsustainable levels. First, there is logging, which continues with savage intensity for various reasons, including commercial forestry, slash-and-burn agriculture, and mining and other developments. It has been estimated that only 9,220km² of suitable forest remains in the whole of the Philippines, and with each pair of birds requiring an average of 68km², that doesn't leave very much space. Second, once the population reaches a certain limit, hunting could come into play as a *coup de grâce*. Third, the Philippine Eagle has a low reproductive output, breeding only once every two years, and the fledglings have an exceptionally long period of dependence upon their parents, lasting a year and a half. Any serious problems during this vulnerable time could become a serious setback to the species as a whole. A fourth problem is that the population is divided over four islands, and thus fragmented. A small number of pairs (unknown) breed on Luzon, two pairs breed on Leyte, six pairs breed on Samar and the rest are on Mindanao.

Very few of the Philippine Eagles that remain occur in protected areas. On Mindanao, Mount Apo and the Katanglad Mountains are both national parks with eagle populations, but this does not prevent the encroachment of slash-and-burn further up their hillsides each year. The Philippines, with an already dense and exploding human population, does not have a strong record of management of its conserved areas and, although the Philippine Eagle is the national bird and formally protected by law, this doesn't hold very much water on the ground.

There is a Philippine Eagle Foundation (PEF) based in Davao City, Mindanao, which performs a unique and valuable service in co-ordinating conservation efforts in the wild and in captive breeding. At present

Left: For much of the time when hunting, the Philippine Eagle simply perches in the forest canopy, quiet and concealed on the lookout for prey.

Below: The Philippine Eagle is entirely dependent on pristine forest dominated by large trees.

the foundation holds 32 individuals, of which 18 are captive-bred – an impressive result. The foundation released its first captive-bred individual into the wild in 2004, but that bird did not last long, electrocuted on a powerline a few months later. Another bird released in 2008 was shot and killed.

However, despite PEF's sterling efforts, the future of the Philippine Eagle remains in the balance, at least in the wild. Even if the captive breeding efforts are a roaring success, the main question is: will there be enough forest left in 10 years to form any kind of proper sanctuary for this magnificent bird?

MARVELLOUS SPATULETAIL

Loddigesia mirabilis

Birders' delight in danger

There are not many birds in the world that generate their own ecotourism industry. But the singularly extraordinary Marvellous Spatuletail is one of the few that does. There are so many birders who want to see this hummingbird that tour companies from Europe and the USA make special trips to see it, and there is an eco-lodge within the species' range that is effectively funded by visitors hoping to catch up with it. And, if the truth be told, very few clients who see the adorned males come back disappointed. This stunning creature lives up to its name.

Part of the bird's appeal can be appreciated only too well in the picture opposite. But that's only a part. In reality the Marvellous Spatuletail is even more extraordinary than any still photograph can capture. When the male is flying, the two rackets of the tail (it is the only hummingbird, and one of the few birds in the world, with only four tail feathers) seem to move around independently, creating an oddly confusing effect. When courting from a perch, males are also able to flick the rackets up so that they dangle in front of their bodies. And when the males step up their display, rapidly flying out mechanically from a perch and back again, the rackets move around so rapidly that the bird looks something like a whirling, spinning top. Males invariably meet together at so-called 'leks' to display communally in front of prospecting females, so the phenomenon is magnified still further and the effect is, quite frankly, mind-blowing.

Interestingly, although the swollen feather ends do play an important part in courtship, it has also been suggested that they might act as a kind of decoy for their brilliantly coloured owners, drawing a predator's attention away from the vulnerable body towards the tail. It sounds plausible, but many a male bird of a variety of species has to trade off its need to 'impress' with personal safety. And nobody will know until somebody removes tails from males and compares their predation rates against unaffected males.

As if its most famous feature wasn't enough to

The map shows parts of South America including the Pacific Ocean, Colombia, Ecuador, Peru, Brazil and Bolivia, with locations such as Punta Chirambirá, BOGOTÁ, Punta Reyes, Punta Manglares, Cabo de San Francisco, Cabo Pascado, QUITO, Cabo Puntilla, La Puntilla, Golfo de Guayaquil, Punta Pariñas, Chiclayo, Iquitos, Rio Negro, Rio Japurá, Rio Amazonas, Rio Napo, Putumayo, Rio Marañón, ACRE, Rio Juruá, Rio Purus, Rio Branco, Punta Salinosó Lachay, LIMA, Lago Titicaca, Arequipa, BOLIVIA, LA PAZ, Cordillera Occidental.

Left: The discs at the end of the Marvellous Spatuletail's tail are used for courtship. Uniquely, males of this species only have four tail feathers in total.

Below: A male in display hovers up and down, and the tail feathers whirl about in dizzying fashion.

confirm the spatuletail's allure, the species is also unusual in other ways. It also has oddly shaped wings that produce a highly distinctive hum unlike those of other hummingbirds, and it also exercises an unexpected feeding technique: rather than hovering in front of flowers to drink the nectar, it often simply perches near a bloom and drinks in a less labour-intensive manner.

The astonishing and fascinating appearance of the Marvellous Spatuletail, however, does not tell the whole story of this hummingbird's mystique to ornithologists. A great deal is also down to its extreme rarity. It has only ever been found in a small and very remote part of northern Peru, cut off from the outside world. Indeed, first collected in 1835 by Andrew Matthews, the Marvellous Spatuletail remained almost unknown in the wild to westerners until the 1960s, when birders came across its headquarters on the eastern slopes of the Rio Utcabamba valley, in the Cordillera de Colán. Even here, though, it is known from only a handful of localities, and seems to be found at low density wherever it does occur.

There is doubtless something in the Marvellous Spatuletail's ecology that limits it to a tiny area, yet nobody has yet worked out exactly what this is. The

MARVELLOUS SPATULETAIL
Loddigesia mirabilis

species locally has a preference for the edges and clearings of humid tropical forest, especially where *Alnus* trees grow above a thick understorey of *Rubus* vegetation. For feeding it seems to have a liking for a red-flowering plant called *Alstroemeria formosissima*, but at least five species of flowers, including some yellow ones, are also known to be visited by spatuletails. In common with other Andean birds, the Marvellous Spatuletail is linked to a narrow altitudinal range between 2,100m and 2,900m, yet none of this actually explains its rarity, for similar conditions apply elsewhere in Peru and, indeed, over many other parts of the Andean chain.

The lack of knowledge about the Marvellous Spatuletail's requirements is deeply disturbing, because these days it seems that its entire known population is under serious threat. For example, by far the best known site to see the bird is a village called Florida beside a lake known as Lago Pomacochas, but in recent years it seems that the birds are becoming more and more difficult to find here. Part of the reason is that the local hillsides have been dramatically denuded over decades, and forest clearance still carries on relentlessly, partly for cash crops such as marijuana. A recent study also found that the locals quite often kill male Marvellous

Opposite: The Marvellous Spatuletail has a liking for red and yellow blooms, especially those of *Alstroemeria formosissima.* Although it feeds at flowers and can hover in the manner of other hummingbirds, it typically perches close to a bloom that is easy to reach.

Left: In common with many South American hummers, this species occurs in rich montane forest exploding with epiphytes and other exotic blooms. The spatuletail only inhabits a narrow altitudinal range between 2,100m and 2,900m.

Spatuletails with slingshots, in the bizarre and unhelpful belief that the little bird's hearts will, if dried and kept, imbue their human owners with greater sexual allure.

All of this is worrying. BirdLife International lists the Marvellous Spatuletail as Endangered, and estimates the population at below 1,000 individuals. It could be many more, of course, if the Marvellous Spatuletail proves simply to be fussy and secretive over a wider region than currently known (and there are odd scattered records from further afield, including an unconfirmed record from Ecuador). On the other hand, it could also be a lot less. On current

evidence the Marvellous Spatuletail is decreasing, its habitat is threatened from all sides and it has nowhere to go.

The Marvellous Spatuletail occurs in the one of the greatest biological treasure troves in the world, the Andean slopes, renowned for an astonishing biodiversity, fabulous scenery and wondrous forms. Few places dazzle the ornithological senses so completely. And no bird within this Shangri-La is quite as opulently adorned as the Marvellous Spatuletail. What a complete tragedy it would be – what a disaster for biodiversity – if this unique hummingbird were soon to pass into history.

PO'OULI

Melamprosops phaeosoma

We hardly knew it ...

There is something unbearably tragic about a bird that becomes extinct very shortly after it was first discovered. That, it seems, is what has happened to a small songbird from the Hawaiian islands called the Po'ouli. Unless some individuals are still hiding away, undiscovered, in the mountains of the island of Maui, it can be recorded that the Po'ouli was only known to science for a pathetic 31 years, from 1973 to 2004.

It is a painful story. The Po'ouli was a unique and special bird, quite different from all its relatives in the once species-rich yet ill-fated Hawaiian honeycreeper family (Drepanididae). Yet, almost unbelievably, the Po'ouli became extinct within the territory and on the watch of the richest and most powerful country in the world, the USA. There is no doubt that its extinction could at least have been postponed by some money and political will, but it was not. The Po'ouli's almost certain demise should bring lasting shame on those who failed to act on its behalf.

The Po'ouli's sad fate could hardly have been imagined back in 1973, when a small group of students from the University of Hawaii embarked on an expedition to the steep, remote mountains of Maui, on the slopes of Mount Haleakala. It was 50 years since the last new bird in the Hawaiian chain had been discovered. Yet they spotted a bird that none of them could recognize: a small, understorey-hugging waif of very wet elfin forest, with a very distinctive combination of short tail, whitish front and bold black face mask. They saw nine birds in all, each part of a mixed-species flock. It soon transpired that the bird was new to science, and was also totally unknown to the indigenous oral tradition. Eventually it was named the Po'ouli by a Hawaiian lexicographer, the name translating as 'dark-headed'.

This new species had been discovered in the midst of turmoil in the fortunes of Hawaiian birds. It was already known that they were under siege. To begin with, deforestation had left them all with nothing much more than pockets of habitat. What was left of the Hawaiian forests and their wildlife were also being undermined by a suite of introduced plants and animals: feral pigs running riot and affecting the vegetation; Black Rats (*Rattus rattus*), cats and the

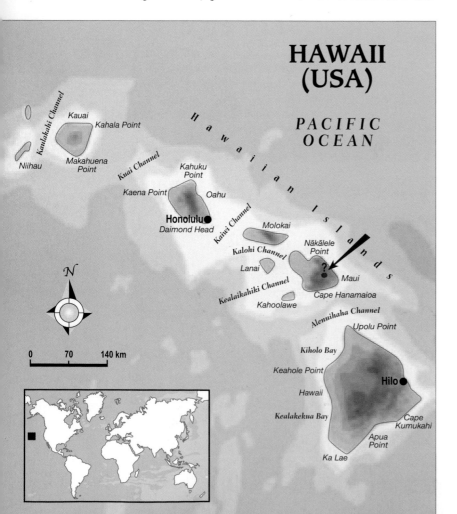

HAWAII
(USA)

PACIFIC
OCEAN

Kaulakahi Channel

Kauai
Kahala Point

Niihau
Makahuena
Point

Kuai Channel

Kahuku
Point

Kaena Point
Oahu

Honolulu
Daimond Head

Kaiwi Channel

Molokai

Nākālele
Point

Kalohi Channel

Lanai

Kealaikahiki Channel

Maui

Cape Hanamaioa

Kahoolawe

Alenuihaha Channel

Upolu Point

Kiholo Bay

Keahole Point

Hilo

Hawaii

Kealakekua Bay

Cape
Kumukahi

Apua
Point

Ka Lae

Hawaiian Islands

N

0   70   140 km

Below: The Po'ouli has not been seen since 2004 and is almost certainly extinct. If so, its demise is nothing short of a scandal.

Small Indian Mongoose (*Herpestes auropunctatus*) raiding nests and eating young; various exotic plants invading the forests. And, to make matters even more serious, mosquitoes introduced since 1800 had infected the native birds with avian pox and avian malaria, drastically reducing their numbers. This onslaught had already wiped out many Hawaiian endemics.

Yet in the excitement surrounding the discovery of the Po'ouli there was at last a rare note of cheer.

Initially, experts made a very rough estimate of about 200 birds in an area totalling only about 1,300ha, and nobody panicked, partly because the area was so remote and potentially undisturbed. It wasn't until 1980, after several birders made reference to a possible decline in numbers, that another survey was undertaken. This found 140 birds, but with a very wide margin of error. Then, in 1986, with greater interest and concern being generated for Hawaiian forest birds generally, some money was given for a

PO'OULI
Melamprosops phaeosoma

more intensive study of the Po'ouli, and the Hanawi Natural Area Reserve (30km²) was designated within the Haleakala National Park

The results of the research were both fascinating and worrying. Fascinating, because it was shown that the Po'ouli was a major consumer of Hawaii's impressive array of native land snails, the only indigenous bird on the islands with such a specialization. Worrying, because the part of the forest where the birds lived was being degraded by the activities of feral pigs – they were destroying the understorey on which the Po'ouli depended. It was later also shown that an introduced snail, the Garlic Snail (*Oxychilus alliarius*) was finding its way into the

forest and preying on the native land snails.

The researchers also found two Po'ouli nests at this time, high in the branches of a native tree called the ohi'a. It turned out that these were the only nests ever found, and the Po'ouli was now, only 23 years after its discovery, in serious trouble. Two years later a survey showed that the birds had all but disappeared from the western part of their tiny range. In the early 1990s, the upper forests were fenced in to keep feral pigs out, but, as it turned out, this was a case of shutting the stable door after the horse had bolted.

Almost unbelievably, at a time when many Hawaiian forest birds were sliding towards extinction, funding for research dried up, both from the state and from federal sources. The late 1980s to the mid-1990s were probably the last chance to save the Po'ouli, but the opportunity slipped by on a wave of indifference and inertia.

By 1994, funding at last came through for another count of Po'ouli numbers and, catastrophically, it came up with only 10 birds, including some immatures. Worse was to come: by 1997, only three individuals appeared to remain in the Hanawi NAR, each with its own distinct home range, each so far apart that they would not be likely to interact at all. Something had to be done.

All three surviving birds were ringed in the 1997-98 season and their gender determined by DNA analysis of the feathers. It seemed that two females and a male were left. A bold decision was taken to translocate one of the females into the male's home range. It took considerable preparation, so that nothing went wrong with such a precious bird. The idea was trialled with another species of less endangered Hawaiian

Opposite: The mist-shrouded forest that is (or was) home to the Po'ouli. In contrast to most members of its family, the species is a bird of the forest understorey rather than the canopy.

Below: It is thought that the Po'ouli was strongly dependent upon a highly unusual food source - land snails.

honeycreeper, the Maui Alauahio (*Paroreomyza montana*) to see what method of transport was the most suitable to employ. Eventually the conservationists settled upon a small container that would be carried in a rucksack and hiked to the new territory, a 75-minute walk. Thus, on 4 April 2002, a female was duly caught, translocated, fitted with a transmitter and left in the male's territory at nightfall, so that it would roost there and meet up with the male the next day. On the pivotal morning, the female awoke and ungratefully made its way back to its own home range, without ever meeting up with its potential partner.

This was probably the last blow for the Po'ouli. After this failure, it was decided to capture all three of the remaining birds and hope that they would breed in a cage. The first bird was duly captured in September 2004, but it sadly died on 26 November that year. As to the other birds, they were never captured. Indeed, these individuals were never seen again.

So the Po'ouli was found and then lost, all in a short space of time. There is no doubt that there was much to find out about it that we never did. But perhaps we will learn its most important legacy, to treat endangered birds with the importance they deserve.

7 CONTROVERSIES

Conservation is rarely a simple business.

Spix's Macaw

In this section are five examples of where the interests of birds and people collide and sparks fly – and it is not always that the bird comes off worst. All the stories have excited controversy and spawned vast amounts of news print around the world.

Each story highlights various big issues surrounding conservation. For example, where do you draw the line when economic needs and conservation needs are at odds? Just how important is the fate of a bird species? Where does captive breeding fit in with a species' recovery? How much money should you put into a key species, especially when the same sum could have a significant impact elsewhere? How should wild populations be managed when the ecological balance has tipped against them? All of these are the difficult questions that conservationists are finding themselves asking at regular intervals.

There is something quite refreshing about the fact that these stories have hit the headlines. It means that people are interested and that they care. As long as conservation stories continue to matter to people, then the birds and wild places that we all love, at least have some hope for the future.

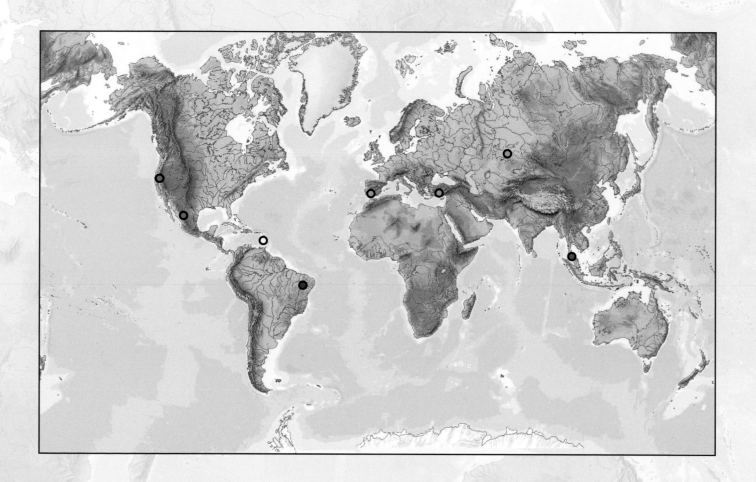

SPOTTED OWL

Strix occidentalis

No hideaway in the forest

Few cases of bird protection have been as controversial and hotly disputed as that of North America's Spotted Owl. This issue has really been a clash of cultures: first, between the passionate environmentalists of modern America and the logging interests that implacably oppose them; and second, on another level, between the economic needs of the modern world and the habitat requirements of the owl itself. These clashes, which have been raging in public for more than 20 years, are still going on today, while in the meantime the owl continues to decline.

The Spotted Owl is a medium-sized predator that occurs in the western half of North America, from British Columbia to Mexico. This is a large range, but everywhere it occurs the Spotted Owl requires old-growth woodland in order to thrive, whether this is coniferous woodland in the north of its range or oak-dominated stands in the south. It is therefore a fussy species in its ecological requirements. Where the owl has been most studied in the coniferous forests of the north-west, it strongly prefers trees that are at least 200 years old. Such tall, multi-layered forests provide all the owl's needs: plenty of nest-site platforms (including large hollows, stick nests of raptors, accumulations of branch debris or abandoned squirrel dreys), lots of small mammals or birds to eat, especially wood rats (*Neotoma* spp.), flying squirrels (*Glaucomys* spp.) and, apparently, the odd smaller owl), plenty of cool sites to roost by day and, overall, a diverse temperature gradient within the microclimate of the habitat.

The Spotted Owl's need for the very purest habitats is stark. In one study, 98 per cent of all territories were in prime old-growth woodland, and in another study 90 per cent of all roost sites were confined there. Spotted Owls can be found in forests between 70 and 140 years old, but only then where there are at least some older trees interspersed. Forests that have recently been logged or degraded simply won't do for them. Furthermore, there is evidence that degraded habitats allow the Spotted Owl's enemy, the closely related but much more aggressive Barred Owl (*Strix varia*), to creep in and usurp territories, often killing or even eating the previous occupants.

Left: The exacting requirements of the Spotted Owl are sharply at odds with economic interests in the United States and Mexico.

All the research done on the species – and it is almost certainly the most intensely studied owl in the world, with more than 1,000 recent scientific papers devoted to it – confirms that the Spotted Owl simply cannot tolerate much alteration of its habitat. And that, of course, means that the cutting down of old-growth forests is essentially a death sentence for any owls that happen to be present.

Unfortunately, logging over parts of the owl's range is very big business indeed. The tallest, oldest trees that the owl cherishes most are of the very highest economic value, with large profits to be made, putting intense pressure on the habitat. To add spice to the plot, in the north-western forests the logging industry is a way of life. Jobs and livelihoods depend on it, and its lifestyle and skills have been passed down the generations, with a distinctive culture to go with it. Not surprisingly, people don't take kindly to losing

SPOTTED OWL
Strix occidentalis

their livelihoods for the sake of an obscure and high-maintenance owl.

So, as soon as conservationists realized that the Spotted Owl was disappearing back in the early 1970s and wished to do something about it, it was only a matter of time before any action put them on a collision course with powerful local industries. The story of the battle to save the Spotted Owl has been riddled with legal wrangling, bad feeling and, latterly, political inertia. What follows is very much a shortened and summarized version of the whole sorry mess.

Alerted by the conservation movement, in 1982 the US Fish and Wildlife Service took a look at the status of the Spotted Owl and decided against listing it as threatened. They repeated this ridiculous feat in 1987 but, in 1988, the first proper blow was struck on behalf of the owl: an action plan was put forward to protect a series of localities in the north-west where it occurred. Although the plan itself was inadequate, by 1990 the Spotted Owl was officially designated as threatened under the US Endangered Species Act.

This designation led to increased funding for research into the owl's needs, and engendered more recovery plans designed to help the species. In 1991 logging in national forests was banned, although the ban was frequently flouted. In 1994, with the situation still unsatisfactory, the Clinton administration put forward the Northwest Forest Plan, which aimed to protect 16 million acres from logging, while allowing the industry to continue in some prime areas. Despite some allowances on their side, this caused the logging industry to see red, citing the death of a lifestyle. It was predicted that some 30,000 people would lose

their jobs. Sawmills hung up Spotted Owl effigies and company employees put stickers on their cars saying such things as 'Kill a Spotted Owl – Save a Logger' – indeed, some persons went out with guns to do exactly that. Many in local industry considered that the citing of the Spotted Owl was an abuse of the Endangered Species Act, and several times species management efforts were stalled in the courts. Opponents of the Spotted Owl continued to argue that the species was not as rare as was being suggested.

Some of the reaction of the logging industry was disingenuous to say the least. Already the lifestyle was dying, for economic reasons that had nothing to do with owls. Some estimates suggested that the industry had a maximum of 30 years left in it. But admittedly, when your lifestyle is threatened it is difficult to take the long view. And there is no doubt that the Spotted Owl has indeed cost jobs.

One of the problems has been that many of the conservation packages suggested simply don't do enough to preserve the owl, while at the same time they do affect the logging industry. Unfortunately, the main outcome to this has been a stalemate. To keep a healthy population of owls, you need to preserve a great deal of forest, and this seems to be too politically difficult to do. The most recent action plan for the Spotted Owl was put forward as long ago as 1992, yet has never been formally accepted by the US Department of the Interior. So, while people wrangle, the owl's prospects do not seem to have improved.

As yet this species is not in danger of extinction. It is officially in the category of Near Threatened, with a total of 15,000 pairs across its huge range. The Mexican race is probably fairly stable, although all the

Left: The Spotted Owl prefers forests made up from trees that are at least 200 years old, such as these Giant Sequioas in California.

Below: Essentially a deep forest bird, the Spotted Owl hunts by watching for prey from a perch at night, and dropping silently on to anything that it sees or hears. This is a Mexican Spotted Owl, which has paler plumage than the birds on the Pacific coast.

populations in the US are declining and the species has almost disappeared from its small range in Canada. However, the case is important. The Spotted Owl has become a symbol: to conservationists it is a symbol of the preservation of forests; to money men and lumberjacks it is a pain. Both sides have valid points. What the case of the Spotted Owl ultimately asks is: just how far should we go to preserve our environment? Where do we draw the line? Where must economic necessities and environmental necessities meet? The fight for the future of the Spotted Owl is, in microcosm, a case study for all conservation.

WHITE-HEADED DUCK

Oxyura leucocephala

An unplanned crossing of paths

If you are a rare species and need to survive, it can be important that you are attractive. If you don't believe this statement, just take the case of the White-headed Duck.

The White-headed Duck is a curious-looking bird – an ugly duck, you might say. It is small, dumpy and heavy-bodied and with a strangely swollen blue bill. The head is white in the male, but the rest of the plumage is an unremarkable chestnut brown. With dull colours and an odd, not very streamlined shape, nobody would ever describe the White-headed Duck as the most beautiful bird they had ever seen.

Of course, this is irrelevant to the ducks themselves, for which people's value judgements mean nothing. But when it comes to attractiveness to the opposite sex, you will agree that this is very important. White-headed Ducks absolutely must be attractive to White-headed Ducks; otherwise the species is in trouble.

Above: The White-headed Duck is one of a small tribe of ducks known as 'stifftails'. The tails are used as rudders when the birds are feeding underwater. The swollen bill is used to strain animal and plant particles from the ooze at the bottom of ponds.

And surprisingly, this is the trouble. White-headed Ducks are having a crisis. The species is under threat from interbreeding with a closely related species, the Ruddy Duck (*Oxyura jamaicensis*). When the two species mix, male Ruddy Ducks are socially dominant over pure White-headeds during courtship, meaning that the females preferentially copulate with them. The display of the Ruddy Duck seems to overpower everything that a male White-headed can do – and it is certainly remarkable. To attract females, male Ruddy Ducks beat their breasts with their large bills several times in quick succession: the extremely dense plumage on the breast holds air, with the result that the beating blows bubbles – surely an irresistible sight. The result is that, little by little, White-headed females are preferring the colonists from across the Atlantic, and fertile hybrids are diluting the pure population of White-headed Ducks.

You might say: why should this matter, if the ducks cannot help themselves? Well, it matters because of one thing. Ruddy Ducks and White-headed Ducks should normally never meet. White-headed Ducks are extremely patchily distributed from Western Europe through to Russia and the Indian Subcontinent, occurring on shallow, often temporary lakes with thick fringing vegetation. The Ruddy Duck is a North American species that mainly breeds on similarly shallow freshwater lakes. It is highly unlikely that Ruddy Ducks could ever make it naturally to Europe, or that White-headed Ducks could make the journey across the Atlantic in the opposite direction.

However, the Ruddy Duck is found in Western Europe. It was introduced by accident in the 1950s. Three pairs were imported to the Wildfowl and Wetlands Trust's world-famous facility at Slimbridge, in Gloucestershire, in 1948, with a view to breeding them in captivity. This was found to be difficult, since although the birds laid plenty of eggs (slightly more than most ducks), it proved hard to rear the chicks by hand, as was the normal practice. The solution was to leave the parent to do the work. Unfortunately, this

153

WHITE-HEADED DUCK
Oxyura leucocephala

meant that some juvenile Ruddy Ducks escaped through the safety net of having their wings pinioned, allowing them to fly free into a land of opportunity in western England. From a series of similar episodes, a feral population began to build up in the 1960s, and between 1975 and 1990 the population increased tenfold. By 2003 there were about 4,000 birds.

Had the Ruddy Ducks confined themselves to Britain, they would have remained harmless curiosities, appreciated by the local birdwatchers and ignored by worried conservationists. However, by 1990 they had already begun to spread their wings and turn up in other European countries, probably meeting up with escaped birds from Holland and elsewhere. Inevitably they soon moved south and began intruding upon the nearest population of White-headed Ducks in Spain. Within a few years hybrids had been recorded.

These Ruddy Ducks were meeting a truly beleaguered and ragged remnant. The Old World's White-headed Duck had already suffered from habitat loss, hunting (it doesn't easily escape from wildfowlers) and egg collection, its European population plummeting from thousands at the beginning of the 20th century to just a few hundreds of individuals. Overall, throughout the world, it was already becoming rare, with no more than perhaps 10,000–15,000 individuals remaining. The Ruddy Duck problem was a further blow to its prospects.

By the time that the Ruddy Duck had bred in six European countries and been seen in 20 of them, the conservationists had decided to step in on behalf of its weakened rival. A number of suggestions were made about how to sort the problem out, but in the end only one solution was considered to be completely effective: to cull Ruddy Ducks in Europe until there were simply none left.

This was a bold, courageous decision. Scientifically, it was flawless. Clearly, if the Ruddy Duck was invading Europe so decisively, there was no way that it was going to avoid the large, crucial populations of White-headed Ducks in their strongholds in Turkey, Russia and Kazakhstan. There was also no way that it was going to yield to conservationists' wishes by avoiding hybridizing with its sibling species. At some point the Ruddy Duck's march would be unstoppable; once that happened, and it was impossible in practice to shoot the birds out, the extinction of the White-headed Duck as a valid species would probably become inevitable.

The arguments were pretty much irresistible, but

in practice the plan to cull the Americans was explosively controversial. Opposition reached its zenith in Britain, where the Ruddy Duck was fairly common and popular. Many people objected to shooting in principle, preferring to let the birds get on with their own conflict. The main driving force behind the cull was seen to be the Royal Society for the Protection of Birds, and thousands of its members resigned in protest. The general public were aghast; Britain is known for its emotional and often sentimental love for animals, and for most the idea of killing a defenceless, handsome little duck with too much sex appeal was too much for many nature lovers. The furore raged for a number of years and, indeed, it rages still.

At present the culling initiative is a work in progress that seems to be having the desired effect: by

Opposite: White-headed Ducks are among the most aquatic of all ducks, rarely taking wing. However, they and their relative the Ruddy Duck do migrate, and this leads to problems when the species meet.

Above: The choosy female White-headed Ducks reportedly mate preferentially with introduced Ruddy Ducks, leading to fears that their species could interbreed out of existence.

the summer of 2009 the Ruddy Duck was down to a few hundred individuals in the UK. But there is still a long way to go if the culling is to have been of any value: the continental population must also be eradicated, or else it will not only continue to threaten the White-headed Duck but also eventually reinvade Britain. Meanwhile, the severe reaction against the cull by animal lovers does prove one thing: it pays to be good-looking.

GRENADA DOVE

Leptotila wellsi

The last resort?

What is more important – the economic benefit afforded by a holiday resort for the very rich; or the protection of a unique, Critically Endangered bird? For all the readers of this book, this is hopefully a no-brainer. Economic benefits are fickle things, and all around the world there are hundreds of thousands of holiday resorts (and they often look startlingly

similar wherever they are). But only on the small West Indian island of Grenada do you find the Grenada Dove.

It is a medium-sized, soft-coloured dove with brown back and wings, pale creamy belly and ash-grey crown, offset by a red eye-ring. It occurs in dry, thorny scrub woodlands on its small island home at elevations up to 150m, relying on areas with quite a closed canopy and a mixture of patches of bare ground and thick vegetation. The Grenada Dove was

Below: The Grenada Dove is the Caribbean country's National Bird, and an icon of conservation.

probably once found in many places around the main island's 440km², and perhaps on some offshore islands, too, but it was always a rare bird with a low population. The ravages of development just made a scarce species scarcer, and by 1977 it had disappeared from the north of the island, leaving all the birds in the west and south-west. By the beginning of the 1990s there were fewer than 100 individuals left. In other words, the Grenada Dove is a Critically Endangered species.

Up until recently, however, it seemed that the government of Grenada and its islanders had begun to recognise this unique part of their heritage and become somewhat proud of their own dove. It was made the country's national bird in 1991. Since then it has regularly featured on stamps, is the focus of environmental education in schools and is seen depicted around the island on pictures, names and logos. In 1996, worried about the Grenada Dove's diminishing numbers, the government delineated a national park, Mount Hartman, in the south of the island specifically to protect the bird. Mitigating against continued development on the rest of the island and recognizing this area as the species' main stronghold, it was a move that was applauded by environmentalists and earned the island some grants from the World Bank.

However, 10 years later something extraordinary happened. In an unprecedented move, the government of Grenada decided to de-gazette the Mount Hartman National Park and adjoining estate and sell the area off to a hotel development company called Four Seasons Hotels and Resorts. The dove's habitat would have been scarred by more than 200

villas, a further 100 other hotel units and an 18-hole golf course. In many parts of the world national parks are abused and their boundaries ignored, and thousands exist only on paper, but this brazen act of executive vandalism was something new to many conservationists. Some equated the move to selling off the country's own crown jewels.

The motive was, as is often the case, economic. Grenada is a small island, and the Mount Hartman

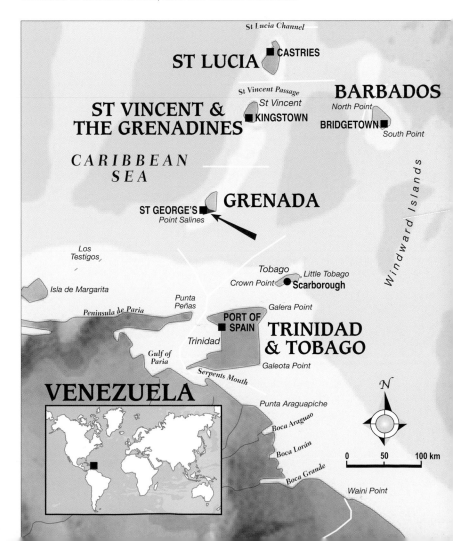

GRENADA DOVE
Leptotila wellsi

area is one of the most scenic remaining on the island, with agreeable sea views. The island's economy had been hit hard by Hurricane Ivan in 2004. But whatever sympathy one might have for a government facing hard decisions was completely quashed by the sneaky way that it went about its business. From the start neither it nor Four Seasons were forthcoming about their plans. In November 1996 they produced an Environmental Impact Assessment of such disgracefully poor quality and

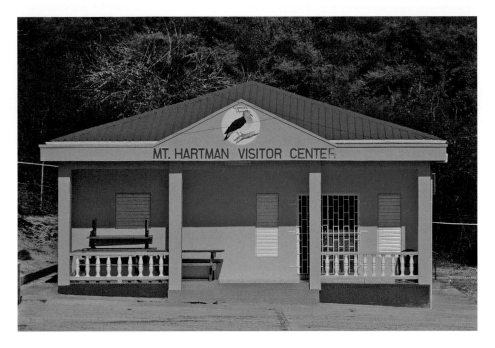

Opposite: The dry, thorny scrub woodland where most Grenada Doves now occur. In the past, the species probably occurred in other habitats.

Left: For now Mount Hartman has both doves and tourists – and sometimes they meet up.

flagrant bias that it engendered both an outcry and well-deserved derision – it lacked, for example, an actual count of Grenada Dove territories, underplayed the site's importance to the species and, in contravention of normal practice, did not even countenance any alternative development proposals that might have had a smaller effect on the doves. Furthermore, in 2007 the Government claimed that the environmental lobby were being alarmist and basing their fears on what was merely a preliminary design. While conservationists were protesting against the development, aerial photographs showed that parts of the site had already been bulldozed in the precise configuration of the original proposals' plans.

Happily, these underhand tactics turned out to be own goals, prompting bad publicity for the Four Seasons developers and making the government look dishonest. Caught red-handed, both constituencies began to show a concern for the Grenada Dove that had hitherto been lacking. They commissioned a full census of doves (which, of course, they should have done at the start) and, sure enough, it showed not just that more than half the existing Grenada Doves depended on the Mount Hartman area (they had originally claimed 22 per cent), but also that the original plan would have had a devastating effect on the fragile dove population.

After much wrangling, the parties have now moved towards a settlement that could yet benefit both the Grenada Dove and the economy. There will still be a tourist development, but the number of villas has been greatly reduced and the national park has been redesigned so that the best dove habitat will now all be in one block rather than several, and this area will encompass 50 of the 58 territories known in the area. The proposal also includes areas for potential habitat restoration, and the government has made a public commitment to protect land at another site, Beauséjour on the west coast (with seven males), by declaring a national park there. Meanwhile, Four Seasons will fund a trapping programme to try to control mongooses, cats and rats, which are thought to predate dove fledglings.

Although the Grenada Dove is still Critically Endangered and the population still stands at the frighteningly low figure of around 100 individuals (which are vulnerable to devastation caused by a severe hurricane, for instance), it is now possible to view the outcome with a degree of satisfaction. The case of the Grenada Doves shows that pressure can work. Governments will always have weasel ways, but they don't always win.

SPIX'S MACAW

Cyanopsitta spixii

A collectors' item

There are few stories of impending extinction more depressing and calamitous than that of the gorgeous Spix's Macaw. The fact that there are any of these parrots alive today is quite extraordinary, and there is even a recent glimmer of hope that the species might yet survive for a few more years. But don't bet on it.

The Spix's Macaw story has many human villains: mainly trappers and, especially, bird collectors. But the reason that the bird is now almost spent is actually more prosaic, and falls in line with a good many of the other species in this book. Spix's Macaw is a real habitat specialist, and its extinction has essentially been caused by the almost complete destruction of its preferred fragile environment. It only ever occurred in a small area of Brazil in gallery woodland alongside the Rio São Francisco and its tributaries. It depended completely upon the presence of large, mature Caraiba trees (*Tabebuia caraiba*) in which it made its nest, and it fed mainly on a small suite of fruits, mainly from the trees *Jatropha* and *Cnidoscolus*. The Caraiba trees typically grow on land that is ideal for maize cultivation, and rapid human settlement meant that the macaw's habitat was destroyed very quickly. Nowadays there is estimated to be less than 30km² of suitable woodland left.

Spix's Macaw lurched into the scientific sphere without ceremony or much recognition. Johann Baptist von Spix came across the bird alongside the banks of the Rio São Francisco in April 1819, but he had no idea that it was a new species, instead believing that he had found a new population of the equally blue Hyacinth Macaw (*Anodorhynchus hyacinthus*). The species was not described formally for another 13 years, and it then disappeared from view for the rest of the century.

Indeed, there are hardly any historical records of wild Spix's Macaws. The next one after the bird's discovery seems to have been in June 1903, more than 80 years later, and the next after that in 1923. Incredibly, the bird then disappeared from the scientific logbook until 1974. It was not until 1985 that an expedition was mounted to try to re-find the bird in its natural habitat, and by then there were only five

Left: An historic photograph of the last Spix's Macaw ever seen in the wild. It disappeared some time after October 2000.

Below: The last fragments of Spix's Macaw's habitat, dominated by Caraiba trees, are under increasing pressure from humans.

individuals left. Such chronic absence of a species from the scientific record is exceptionally unusual.

A quite different constituency to the explorers and zoologists had, however, been well aware of the bird and its increasing rarity during these wilderness years. While it was almost unknown in the wild, the beautiful macaw occasionally found its way into captivity, both in zoos and, especially latterly, in private collections. Indeed, during the 1970s and early 1980s there was evidently a steady trade in the increasingly valuable birds, with more than 20 taken from the wild and exported into the black market.

The 1985 discovery of just five individuals, together with the publicity surrounding it, did nothing to deter poaching; far from it, it probably increased the rewards for the unscrupulous (by now Spix's Macaws were fetching US$20,000 a bird, more than their weight in gold). In defiance of the law and the authorities, one of the five birds was killed, one disappeared, and the other three were collected by a single dealer at regular intervals up to the beginning of 1988

ALGERIAN NUTHATCH

Sitta ledanti

The secret of Djebel Babor

If you ever wished to discover new species of bird for science, there are certain places, and countries, where you would have a better chance than most to fulfil your dream. Colombia and Vietnam are two recent hotspots, but there are a surprising number of thick tropical forests and remote mountain ranges in the world where it might still happen, even today, for the dedicated searcher.

However, there are definitely some places where it cannot be worth looking. In North America or in Europe you have rather little hope of finding something new. These parts of the world have been well studied for more than two centuries, and it seems pretty inconceivable that anything truly novel, at least in Europe, could have possibly gone undetected up to now. Before 1975 you would have said the same thing for North Africa, just a stone's throw from the bustling continent of Europe. The Maghreb has a distinctive, sophisticated culture and a similar long history of exploration. What could be found there, you might think, has been found already.

Any thoughts of sensational discovery would doubtless have been far from Belgian ecologist Jean-Paul Ledant's mind on the afternoon on 5 October 1975, as he settled down to write among the tall forest trees close to the summit of Djebel Babor, a peak of the Petite Kabylie range in northern Algeria. He had only arrived in the country the year before, to take up a job as a forestry assistant with the Institut National Agronomique. Now, just a short time later, he was part of an expedition to study the montane forest on this peak, a relict stand dominated by Algerian Fir (*Abies numidica*), Atlas Cedar (*Cedrus atlantica*) and, further down, Atlas Oak (*Quercus faginea*). Ledant was on a job, and not there to look at birds.

However, as he was writing he became distracted by a tapping sound above him. Almost immediately he spotted the source, a small nuthatch with a black cap and an eyestripe, working the tree trunks not far above him. It wasn't a spectacular bird to look at, but

Below left: A female Algerian Nuthatch at its nest hole. Leading a quiet life in the treetops somehow concealed this species from discovery until 1975.

Below: More prominent black on the crown and eye-stripe identify this bird as a male Algerian Nuthatch.

it reminded Ledant of the Corsican Nuthatch (*Sitta whiteheadi*), a species from its namesake island a few hundred kilometres away in the Mediterranean. Ledant was puzzled. What was it doing here?

If Ledant was confused, his companions on the expedition, Dirk Raes and Paul Jacobs, who had remained at their base camp further down the slope while Ledant was writing, were incredulous when the Belgian recounted his discovery. Their immediate thought must have been that the 24-year-old was mistaken. They weren't aware of any nuthatch of any kind occurring in Algeria and, if Ledant was right, he would have stumbled upon something extraordinary.

If the two men harboured any doubts, these were soon dispelled the following morning, however, when

Ledant successfully found the strange nuthatch again. Frustratingly, however, the expedition's goal was to study the trees of the forest, not the nuthatch, and despite the excitement that they must have felt, they needed to return to the task in hand. Their time on the summit ran out before they could make any further useful observations.

ALGERIAN NUTHATCH
Sitta ledanti

The team returned to Djebel Babor in December 1975. Although they undertook this time to re-find their bird, the trip was an almost comical failure. The summit of the 2,000-metre mountain is a harsh environment, especially in mid-winter, when it is frequently blanketed with up to 4m of snow, and the group spent more time trying to stay alive than anything else; they didn't see a single nuthatch. However, not to be outdone, Ledant and Jacobs trudged up yet again in April 1976 and this time, after enduring more than 48 hours of appalling weather and once again fighting their way through heavy snowdrifts, they finally made the definitive observations that clinched the Algerian Nuthatch as a previously undescribed species. It was formally described a few months later, named after Ledant, in a special edition of the French ornithological journal *Alauda*.

Amazingly, during the period between those spring observations and the first official release of the news (in the newspaper *Le Monde* in July 1976), the hitherto unknown nuthatch of Djebel Babor was 'discovered' again, this time by a Swiss naturalist named Eric Burnier. Completely unaware of what had happened a few months before, he independently found the nuthatch in June 1976 close to the summit. Having excitedly made detailed notes and sketches, his heart must have sunk to his boots when he found out that his observations were not new after all. He had missed out on finding a new species by a mere eight months.

Since those heady days in the mid-1970s any delight that the Algerian Nuthatch had given to ornithologists had quickly become overshadowed by concern. The new species was obviously very rare, and early population estimates came up with a mere 80 birds in total. The core area for the nuthatch was only 250m in extent and, furthermore, the special woodlands where it lived were being degraded by overgrazing of the understorey, reducing the habitat diversity on which the species depended. Fire was also a potential hazard in such a minute area.

For the next 14 years the situation remained precarious. Then, in June 1989, a new population was discovered in another forest on the Petite Kabylie. The Guerrouch Forest was a much larger tract of land with, it turned out, many more nuthatches (several hundred) and, although the birds were still found at high elevation, they seemed to have less exacting habitat requirements than the Djebel Babor population. The situation eased further the following year when small numbers were revealed in two other nearby forests, the Tamentout and Djimla Forests. All of these localities are between 5km and 30km from each other and, despite intensive searching all over the Petite Kabylie, it seems as though there are no further Algerian Nuthatches anywhere else. Nowadays the best estimate for the Algerian Nuthatch's world population is just under 1,000 individuals, and the largest block of them, in Guerrouch, is protected within Taza National Park.

So it looks as though, for now, Jean-Paul Ledant's nuthatch is in no great danger of extinction. But one thing about its discovery, even 30 years later, still seems hard to grasp, almost inexplicable. How on earth was this distinctive bird overlooked for so long? After all, the Petite Kabylie range is neither especially high nor very remote (close to the coast and not far from Algiers, the capital). People – birdwatchers or

Left: Male Algerian Nuthatch carrying food. This is the only nuthatch species present in its range.

Below: The relict montane forests of the Petite Kabylie range that kept a secret for so long.

natural history enthusiasts – must have noticed the nuthatch, or at least heard it, when they hiked in these hills long before 1975. How did they miss it? And additionally, when the nuthatch had been discovered, why did it take 14 years to discover the other populations so close by, when these woodlands would surely have been the first place to look for the bird? It seems barely comprehensible.

And so, perhaps, there's a lesson to be learned here. Perhaps there's an incredible discovery still to be made even today – and not far from where you are reading this book?

NECHISAR NIGHTJAR

Caprimulgus solala

Out on a Limb?

Of all the bird discoveries of the last 20 or so years, few can be more extraordinary than that of the Nechisar Nightjar of Ethiopia. The following tale is, in many ways, a cautionary one. Yet it is also a celebration of the ability of wild creatures to be tantalizing and messy, and hard to place in convenient boxes.

The story begins on the night of 3 September 1990. A multidisciplinary team was nearing the end of a three-month survey of Nechisar National Park, in southern Ethiopia, a wild and sparsely populated location deep in East Africa's Rift Valley. On this particular evening, a group of five ornithologists decided to take a long night drive in order to make detailed records of the area's nightjars. These insectivorous nocturnal birds often rest on roads, apparently because of the warmth that compact surfaces retain, and nightjars are easy to spot in car headlights because of the bright reflections of their eyes. The team set off at 21.15 in the evening and immediately began making sightings of the birds.

The night drive went well, and the five observers eventually logged 36 different nightjars, of four definite species. During the period between nightfall and 01.00 on 4 September, they also found a road-killed bird, which they decided to keep for identification. Unfortunately it was badly squashed and decomposed. It had lain there somewhere between two days and a week, and as they tried to recover it from the soil, the tail, which had white-tipped feathers, blew away in the wind. However, they were able to retain a wing for analysis.

When they got round to examining the wing the next morning, the biologists were surprised that its pattern did not seem to fit with any of the species they had seen: the Slender-tailed (*Caprimulgus clarus*), Star-spotted (*C. stellatus*), Sombre (*C. fraenatus*) and Donaldson Smith's Nightjars (*C. donaldsoni*). It was quite considerably larger and longer. They checked the literature available in the field but, puzzlingly, they could not find any other species that had a

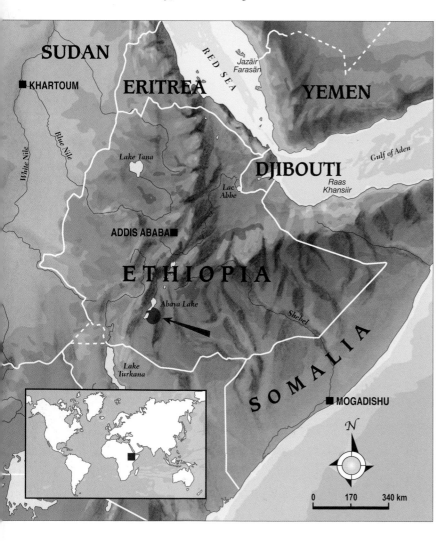

Below: The famous (or infamous) wing that forms the incomplete type specimen of the Nechisar Nightjar.

HOODED GREBE

Podiceps gallardoi

Shot to stardom ...

The Hooded Grebe is a delightful waterbird found in southern Argentina and Chile. In breeding plumage it is a striking grebe, with sharply contrasting black-and-white plumage and a brilliant chestnut crest on its crown. Given a decent view in the austral summer it would be hard to mistake it for any other bird. And where it occurs it tends to be found at high density, in colonies out in the open on shallow lakes. So it is indeed remarkable that the Hooded Grebe managed to elude scientists completely until the comparatively recent date of 1974. And it so happens that it could have remained undetected for a good deal longer than that, had it not been for a strangely unlikely set of circumstances.

The key character in the story is the distinguished Argentinian film-maker, photographer and biologist Maurice Rumboll. In 1974 he happened to be studying the migratory behaviour of geese, and his work took him to many remote locations in southern Argentina. One fateful autumn day he and fellow biologist Edward Shaw decided to visit the Laguna de los Escarchados, a 3km-long lake at an altitude of 700m in the extreme south-west of the country, in the foothills of the Andes. When they got there the lagoon was full of birds, including high numbers of both White-tufted (*Rollandia rolland*) and Silvery Grebes (*Podiceps occipitalis*). It happened that, besides looking for geese, Shaw and Rumboll also had another purpose at the lake: Shaw was a student ornithologist and Rumboll had promised to show him how to prepare a study specimen. And since there were plenty of grebes on the laguna, Rumboll went and shot the nearest one.

Still unaware of anything amiss, Shaw and Rumboll put the corpse into their vehicle and returned to the National Museum of Natural History in Buenos Aires. It was only when they finally got around some time later to examining the specimen that the penny dropped. They looked at the specimen there before them, suddenly utterly incredulous. This was no Silvery Grebe, as they had assumed; this was a species they couldn't recognize at all! Of all the birds that Rumboll might have shot for the routine purpose of specimen preparation, it turned out that he had chosen a hitherto unknown species, just by chance in

Left: The stunning Hooded Grebe. How was it missed for so long?

Below: Some Patagonian lagoons teem with birds. These are Black-necked Swans (*Cygnus melancoryphus*), Chiloe Wigeons (*Anas sibilatrix*) and White-winged Coots (*Fulica leucoptera*).

HOODED GREBE

Podiceps gallardoi

Below: Hooded Grebes have proved to exhibit some highly unusual – and ruthless – breeding behaviour.

ed
The
years

day
have no
ooner
re
mble to
ly what
anakin. At
tive species
forest just a
most
ked at 250
he type
tion Area,
y for it in
ements on
a popular local
ment for parks

en restricted to
, it would now be
locality was
water-park,
all patch of forest
rkably, manages to
of people.
oil company,
d in the region
n movement
s to finance intensive
ipe Manakin in

nearby habitat. These initiatives were successful, and at present there are known to be about 800 birds scattered over a region of about 28km².

A thorough study has put some flesh on the life history of the Araripe Manakin. It is, in common with most members of its family (manakins, Pipridae), a bird of the lower and middle tier of the forest, where it feeds almost entirely on small fruits (manakins are major dispersers of tropical forest trees). Its habitat is tall, moist forest with an abundance of vines, and every nest that has been found so far has been in vegetation overhanging streams. The birds breed during the rains, and when the times of these vary, so does the breeding season. Presumably, in common with other manakins, the female performs all nesting and incubation duties, although for much of the year the species is seen in pairs.

Whatever we now know about it, the Araripe Manakin's future is still precarious, and the species is currently listed as Critically Endangered. Just to give an idea of its vulnerability: in 2005 an area where the manakins occur was ravaged by a large forest fire. Seven known nests were threatened, and it was only heroic action by the manakin research team (that included Weber Silva) in tackling the flames that prevented the nests from being destroyed altogether. This incident, in which the workers put their own lives at risk, shows how just a single disastrous event could almost destroy the population of a bird like the Araripe Manakin.

There is, however, a good deal of support for this striking species. Aside from the grants received to study it, the Araripe Manakin has also attracted financial help and very public accolades from the

this remote but essentially unremarkable location.

Even back in 1974, the discovery of a new species brought as much concern as delight. The very fact that the bird had never been seen before suggested that it might have an extremely restricted distribution – even, perhaps, a population confined to this single small lake. A follow-up survey in 1975 showed that the birds could be relocated, and came up with a count of 126 individuals. However, this survey was undertaken in December, and during the time that Rumboll was on-site, now joined by renowned grebe specialist Professor Robert Storer, some of the grebes flew off as the lake began to freeze. Clearly, the birds went elsewhere for the winter, but where? Checks on nearby waters proved fruitless.

It wasn't until three years later that a few extra grebes were found on two small wetlands close to Laguna de los Escharchados, showing that the birds were not completely confined to one single lake. Then in 1981 the species was found breeding on another lake 120km to the north, taking the world population towards the 300 mark. Disaster followed. The early 1980s showed a serious plunge in numbers, with both colonies suffering severe predation at the nest from Kelp Gulls (*Larus dominicanus*). In the absence of any more discoveries, the world population suddenly fell to 45 birds.

It was only then when, seemingly on the brink of extinction only 10 years after being discovered, that the real Hooded Grebe finally revealed itself. The true core population, still hidden after all these years, was finally found to be yet further to the north, in a region known as the Meseta de Strobel. This was an area of small basaltic lakes scattered across a remote, harsh

plateau 800–1,200m above sea level. Happily, in 1984 no less than 1,500 pairs of Hooded Grebes were discovered here. Later, still more birds materialized on other Patagonian plateaux in the area, until by 1997 there were estimated to be up to 5,000 in all. Some showed themselves to be wintering on a couple of estuaries on the Atlantic coast of Santa Cruz state, making it still more bewildering that the species wasn't discovered before 1974.

The Hooded Grebe has something of an extreme lifestyle. For much of the year it lives in open, saline lakes, where it feeds on the high concentrations of invertebrates that occur in the absence in such waters of fish. The lakes are cold and windblown. In the breeding season, the Hooded Grebe moves to shallow lakes with dense carpets of Water Milfoil (*Myriophyllum elatinoides*) on the surface, on which the birds nest. However, these carpets are not ideal feeding areas, being too densely vegetated for diving, so the birds rely on a mosaic of open water and milfoil for the successful bringing up of young. Their nesting success is extraordinarily low, a mere 0.12 juveniles per pair per year, one of the lowest for any bird in the world. The main problem is that enough food is hard to come by, and by the time the two chicks have hatched, there might not be enough large snails to sustain the adults themselves to the end of the breeding season. In this case the adults simply leave the lake and abandon their brood to starve. They never raise more than one chick, anyhow; the second bird is simply an insurance policy, and is not fed unless the first one has died. It's a harsh life indeed.

In fact, you could ask how on earth the Hooded Grebe actually survived until 1974 in the first place?

UDZUNGWA FOREST PARTRIDGE
Xenoperdix udzungwensis

T
co
Jac
Jon
Partr
High
detaile
morph
smaller)
character
they prop
marked sul
but genetic
distinct enou
the Rubeho Fo
The two popul

ARARIPE MANAKIN
Antilophia bokermanni

course, they were stunned: this was no Helmet
Manakin, but something very different indeed
Araripe Manakin was described for science tw
later.

There is a recurring theme among present
discoveries or rediscoveries that readers will
doubt have noticed in this book already: no
does a bird show itself for the first time befo
scientists and conservationists have to scra
save it from extinction. This is most certain
has happened in the case of the Araripe M
the time of its first appearance this distinc
seemed to be restricted to a tiny stretch o
square kilometre in extent, and even the
optimistic estimates of its population pea
birds. To make matters worse, although
locality was in an Environmental Prote
there wasn't much legally binding safe
practice, no more than a few pronoun
paper. Unfortunately the area was also
holiday destination, subject to develo
and groups of apartments.

Had the Araripe Manakin truly be
its original square kilometre of fores
on the brink of extinction. The type
indeed developed in 2000 as a large
although the owners have left a sm
intact for the manakin which, rem
hold on there despite the presenc
However, by 2004 a multinationa
British Petroleum, had got involv
through the Brazilian conservati
Aquasis, and it put in large gra
surveys and searches for the

Left: Manakins have wide gapes that enable them to swallow fruit. They eat very little else, and are major dispersers of forest trees.

Below: Araripe Manakins live and breed in the lower and middle storeys of the forest. In 2005 several conservation workers put their own lives at risk to defend several manakin nests from a fierce forest fire.

great broadcaster and naturalist Sir David Attenborough. He has become BirdLife International's 'Species Champion' for the Araripe Manakin, and will help to ensure that the manakin's fate will receive plenty of publicity, both abroad and in Brazil. Already a campaign to take the message of the manakin's plight to local schools, for example, and to local government officials, is well underway. This should help to protect the forest on which this bird depends.

In the end, the trip from obscurity to world fame is probably what will save this glorious bird from extinction.

9 REDISCOVERIES

Missing birds are found again.

New Zealand Storm-petrel

It's a curious fact that, in recent years, it is not the newly discovered species of birds that are really hitting the headlines and capturing the imagination of the birdwatcher on the street – it is the rediscovered ones. Perhaps it is because a new species doesn't have the chance to become famous, making it into the consciousness by having once been lost? Perhaps this is because the new birds are not always box-office? An obscure babbler or warbler in an obscure rainforest, for example, is not always going to ignite passion. But perhaps there is another reason, too? Rediscoveries are cheering. While a new discovery is an event for the lucky few, a rediscovery is for all of us. In a world where we are getting used to losing animals, to see one surviving against the odds is uplifting and refreshing.

The stories presented here are mainly very recent rediscoveries, whose stories are live and active to this day, while one is an older, but very significant event. In contrast to the discoveries in the previous section, which are mostly cases of glorious serendipity, several of these accounts show that a rediscovery can be a case of careful planning and hard work.

The delight of this section is that, almost as soon as you read it, an exciting story is bound to break that will better the accounts given here, by virtue of being more recent and, by implication, more unexpected. Who knows, perhaps some of the birds in the next section would appear here in future editions?

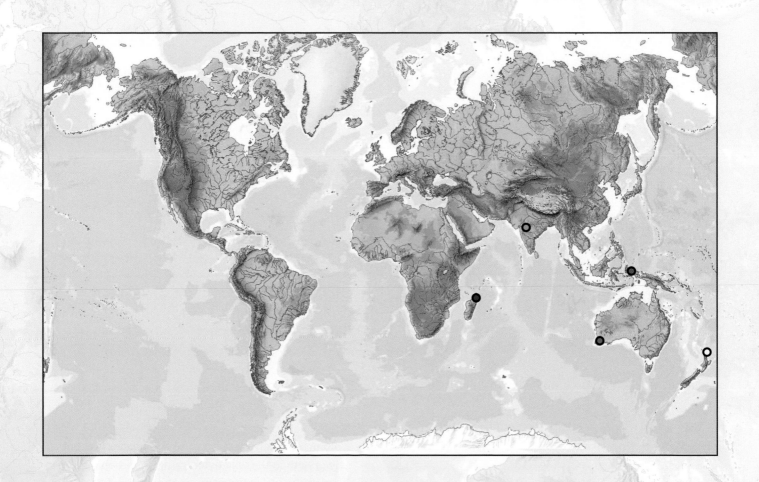

NOISY SCRUB-BIRD
Atrichornis clamosus

by the settlers, a regime aimed at producing good grazing for cattle. However, by removing the density of ground vegetation the change was catastrophic for Noisy Scrub-birds and this, along with large-scale clearing of the bush for agriculture, depleted the population so much that there were no records at all in the first half of the 20th century, despite thorough searches.

In many ways, the memory of the Noisy Scrub-bird might have simply faded away. But in the 1930s Gilbert's copious notes and fascinating diaries, lost for nearly 100 years, were found once again, by a researcher named A.H. Chisholm. They had been kept by the Port Essington expedition organizer, Ludwig Leichhardt, but their historical and scientific significance had been overlooked. However, the finding of the papers allowed for a reappraisal of Gilbert, a man who had a river, a small kangaroo, Gilbert's Potoroo (*Potorous gilberti*), and a bird, Gilbert's Whistler (*Pachycephala inornatus*), named after him. In 1948 a small memorial was erected to Gilbert not far away from where the Noisy Scrub-bird had been discovered more than a century before. And since the scrub-bird seemed to have gone the same way, the monument is dedicated also to the lost 'sweet-voiced bird of the bush'.

Then, in 1961, the Noisy Scrub-bird made its unexpected comeback. It was famously rediscovered at Two Peoples Bay, east of Albany, by some local naturalists. It seems as though the tricky terrain of mountainside and steep gullies had saved the birds from the depredations of changed fire regime. However, the rediscovered population was frighteningly small and vulnerable: only a maximum

of 100 birds, and all on the slopes of Mount Gardner. Indeed, the small population wasn't the only threat. The main problem was that the foot of Mount Gardner had been selected as the site of a large new development.

It is probably fair to say that, up until this point in the early days of the environmental movement, there would still have been every chance that the town would have been built and the Noisy Scrub-bird consigned to extinction. But the world was beginning to change and the scrub-bird became a *cause célèbre*. It was partly the bird's interesting history, and partly the fact that it is an unusual and intriguing species, that made the campaign to save it unstoppable. International pressure from scientists and, eventually, the media, created the bandwagon that eventually saved the obscure but amusingly named skulker.

The campaigners won. The Two Peoples Bay Nature Reserve was formed in 1967 and the town was never built. The Noisy Scrub-bird was carefully protected and studied and, since those heady days of the 1960s, the population has been built up slowly and steadily, not least by several translocations to other areas within the same corner of Western Australia. There are now about 1,000–1,500 individuals in the wild.

In 2004 another highly satisfying course of events brought the story to a neat conclusion. Not far from the site of Gilbert's and the scrub-bird's memorial, another population of scrub-birds was reintroduced to Drakesbrook, in the Darling Range. It is here, at a spot steeped in history, that you can nowadays listen to a Noisy Scrub-bird and contemplate how attitudes to our natural environment have changed.

this remote but essentially unremarkable location.

Even back in 1974, the discovery of a new species brought as much concern as delight. The very fact that the bird had never been seen before suggested that it might have an extremely restricted distribution – even, perhaps, a population confined to this single small lake. A follow-up survey in 1975 showed that the birds could be relocated, and came up with a count of 126 individuals. However, this survey was undertaken in December, and during the time that Rumboll was on-site, now joined by renowned grebe specialist Professor Robert Storer, some of the grebes flew off as the lake began to freeze. Clearly, the birds went elsewhere for the winter, but where? Checks on nearby waters proved fruitless.

It wasn't until three years later that a few extra grebes were found on two small wetlands close to Laguna de los Escharchados, showing that the birds were not completely confined to one single lake. Then in 1981 the species was found breeding on another lake 120km to the north, taking the world population towards the 300 mark. Disaster followed. The early 1980s showed a serious plunge in numbers, with both colonies suffering severe predation at the nest from Kelp Gulls (*Larus dominicanus*). In the absence of any more discoveries, the world population suddenly fell to 45 birds.

It was only then when, seemingly on the brink of extinction only 10 years after being discovered, that the real Hooded Grebe finally revealed itself. The true core population, still hidden after all these years, was finally found to be yet further to the north, in a region known as the Meseta de Strobel. This was an area of small basaltic lakes scattered across a remote, harsh

plateau 800–1,200m above sea level. Happily, in 1984 no less than 1,500 pairs of Hooded Grebes were discovered here. Later, still more birds materialized on other Patagonian plateaux in the area, until by 1997 there were estimated to be up to 5,000 in all. Some showed themselves to be wintering on a couple of estuaries on the Atlantic coast of Santa Cruz state, making it still more bewildering that the species wasn't discovered before 1974.

The Hooded Grebe has something of an extreme lifestyle. For much of the year it lives in open, saline lakes, where it feeds on the high concentrations of invertebrates that occur in the absence in such waters of fish. The lakes are cold and windblown. In the breeding season, the Hooded Grebe moves to shallow lakes with dense carpets of Water Milfoil (*Myriophyllum elatinoides*) on the surface, on which the birds nest. However, these carpets are not ideal feeding areas, being too densely vegetated for diving, so the birds rely on a mosaic of open water and milfoil for the successful bringing up of young. Their nesting success is extraordinarily low, a mere 0.12 juveniles per pair per year, one of the lowest for any bird in the world. The main problem is that enough food is hard to come by, and by the time the two chicks have hatched, there might not be enough large snails to sustain the adults themselves to the end of the breeding season. In this case the adults simply leave the lake and abandon their brood to starve. They never raise more than one chick, anyhow; the second bird is simply an insurance policy, and is not fed unless the first one has died. It's a harsh life indeed.

In fact, you could ask how on earth the Hooded Grebe actually survived until 1974 in the first place?

UDZUNGWA FOREST PARTRIDGE

Xenoperdix udzungwensis

A new species served up

It's amazing what you can find at the bottom of a cooking pot. At the beginning of July 1991, in a camp in the thick forests of the Udzungwa Highlands of south-central Tanzania, four Danish scientists settled down to their evening meal. As they were partaking of their dish, one of them happened to notice a pair of strange feet in the pot of game stew being eaten by the local guides. On examination, it was clear that the feet belonged to a gamebird that was unfamiliar. The scientists were eating what appeared to be a bird unknown to science.

This became a second clue as to the presence of a new species. On their very first day in the forest, two of the scientists had seen a flock of five plump birds shaped like francolins (*Francolinus* spp.), the most typical gamebirds over much of Africa. But these were distinctly different from any francolins they had seen or known about, with striking colours and patterns. At the time of the sighting they had put the discrepancy down to inadequately illustrated field guides. These birds, surely, were the owners of the peculiar feet.

The birds proved to be common in the area, and for the next few months the researchers saw them frequently – in fact, no less than 85 times. But when it came to catching one for a specimen to show the scientific world (as is the requirement for the acceptance of a new species), that was quite a different matter. They might have eaten their quarry unknowingly, but the strange fowl never flew into the scientists' mist-nets and proved itself maddeningly elusive. Eventually, though, with the help of their local guides, two of the birds were snared.

The novelty of the find was quickly established, and the species was described formally two years later. The Udzungwa Forest Partridge, as it was named in English, turned out to be a bird of mainly mountainous evergreen forest, occurring especially along ridges and slopes. It was seen to forage in leaf-litter on the forest floor and consume both seeds and invertebrates. It roosted up in the trees in groups of up to 10 or so. It was found at altitudes between 1,300m and 2,400m and, for a previously unknown species, was both locally common and moderately

widespread at the time of discovery, with a total population estimated at several thousand birds.

Whether or not it was common, however, the Udzungwa Forest Partridge made waves within the scientific community. It turned out that those feet did indeed not exactly fit, at least metaphorically. The Udzungwa Forest Partridge was curiously un-African. The bright rufous colour on the side of the head and on the throat; the grey on the breast and flanks; the wing-linings with contrasting black-and-white – all these features fitted in with equivalent Asian gamebirds, not African ones. The forest partridge thus provided a puzzle – what was an Asian-type gamebird doing in Africa? The question had been asked before when, in 1936, when an explorer by the name of

Above: The striking colours and patterns on the Udzungwa Forest Partridge quickly identified it as a species totally different from the other gamebirds found in the same region.

James Chapin found a bird from the Central African rainforest that was unmistakably a pheasant-type – indeed, a peafowl, the Congo Peafowl (*Afropavo congensis*). The most plausible theory is that the Udzungwa Forest Partridge is a relict from the Miocene era, when an ancient ocean known as the Tethys Sea was briefly closed, allowing interchange between Africa and India. In recent years a true genetic link between the forest partridges and a group of Asian partridges has been proven, suggesting that this is precisely what happened.

UDZUNGWA FOREST PARTRIDGE

Xenoperdix udzungwensis

Opposite: Getting to grips with an enigma – there is a proven genetic link between the Udzungwa Forest Partridges and the gamebirds of Asia.

Left: The forest partridge forages on the leaf-litter of the forest floor.

That wasn't the end of the story, though. Some time after the original discovery, another population of forest partridges was found in the Mafwemiro Forest, in the Rubeho Mountains 150km to the north. These birds were first seen in 2000, and a feather was collected by the indefatigable Tanzanian ornithologist, Jacob Kiure. A few months later in early 2001, he and Jon Fjeldså, who had examined the Udzungwa Forest Partridge a decade before, returned to the Rubeho Highlands and caught three adult birds. They took a detailed description and realized that the birds were morphologically different (for example, they were smaller) and had some different plumage characteristics to the population of Udzungwa. At first they proposed that the Rubeho birds were a well-marked subspecies of the Udzungwa Forest Partridge, but genetic tests soon suggested that the birds were distinct enough to be considered another new species, the Rubeho Forest Partridge (*Xenoperdix obscurata*). The two populations would have been well isolated from one another for millions of years by an area of open plains and a large river.

What is beyond doubt is that both of these forest partridges are now Endangered. Even before it was 'officially' discovered, Udzungwa Forest Partridge was known to be good to eat, and the local people still trap it widely with snares. Large forest mammals also have a taste for partridge, and some wide trails have been cut into the forest by Tanzania National Parks (TANAPA) which allow these predators easier access. The human population is also growing in the area, and this will inevitably put pressure on what forest remains. It is a familiar story.

Hopefully, the Udzungwa and Rubeho Forest Partridges will survive. What with their recent discovery, their Endangered status and their unexpected link with Asian gamebirds, there's no arguing that these birds have scientists in a stew. And that completes a turnaround from the Udzungwa Forest Partridge's original discovery.

ARARIPE MANAKIN

Antilophia bokermanni

International rescue

The story of the Araripe Manakin begins with a chance encounter in a small patch of secondary growth forest in north-east Brazil, and culminates in international concern, large grants and the endorsement of the world's most celebrated conservationist and natural history broadcaster. Perhaps this is the way for new discoveries these days: from complete unknown to world-famous within a few years.

Let's face it, though. The Araripe Manakin was always going to be a star. It is a quite stunning bird, roughly the size of a House Sparrow (*Passer domesticus*) but with improbable smooth, snow-white plumage except for jet-black wings and a cherry-red, forward-pointing crest of dense feathering. The male could not be mistaken for anything else and, indeed, it never was. If you add in the X-factor of extreme rarity, and the curiosity that it somehow managed to evade the eyes of scientists for so long, then you have the right mix for a bird that is going to attract a great

deal of attention.

Perhaps surprisingly, however, the actual discovery of the Araripe Manakin was something of a slow burner. It came as a result of surveys in humid forest on the slope of the Chapada do Araripe, in Ceará province, carried out by two local scientists, Galileu Coelho and Weber Silva, of the Universities of Pernambuco and Ceará respectively. On 19 November 1994 Coelho heard a call that pricked his curiosity: it resembled that of the Helmeted Manakin (*Antilophia galeata*) in tone, but was different. And besides, the humid forest habitat was wrong for this species, which usually occurs in riverine forest within the grassland (cerrado) biome. He failed to locate the caller, however, and went on his way. It wasn't until the following year – indeed almost exactly a year later – that Coelho heard the call again and realized that it was a consistent vocalization: it needed checking. However, again the bird proved elusive and it wasn't until another year later, in December 1996, that Coelho and Weber finally nailed their quarry. They were armed with audio equipment to record the call, and they also made sight records for the first time. Of

ARARIPE MANAKIN
Antilophia bokermanni

course, they were stunned: this was no Helmeted Manakin, but something very different indeed. The Araripe Manakin was described for science two years later.

There is a recurring theme among present-day discoveries or rediscoveries that readers will have no doubt have noticed in this book already: no sooner does a bird show itself for the first time before scientists and conservationists have to scramble to save it from extinction. This is most certainly what has happened in the case of the Araripe Manakin. At the time of its first appearance this distinctive species seemed to be restricted to a tiny stretch of forest just a square kilometre in extent, and even the most optimistic estimates of its population peaked at 250 birds. To make matters worse, although the type locality was in an Environmental Protection Area, there wasn't much legally binding safety for it in practice, no more than a few pronouncements on paper. Unfortunately the area was also a popular local holiday destination, subject to development for parks and groups of apartments.

Had the Araripe Manakin truly been restricted to its original square kilometre of forest, it would now be on the brink of extinction. The type locality was indeed developed in 2000 as a large water-park, although the owners have left a small patch of forest intact for the manakin which, remarkably, manages to hold on there despite the presence of people. However, by 2004 a multinational oil company, British Petroleum, had got involved in the region through the Brazilian conservation movement Aquasis, and it put in large grants to finance intensive surveys and searches for the Araripe Manakin in

nearby habitat. These initiatives were successful, and at present there are known to be about 800 birds scattered over a region of about 28km².

A thorough study has put some flesh on the life history of the Araripe Manakin. It is, in common with most members of its family (manakins, Pipridae), a bird of the lower and middle tier of the forest, where it feeds almost entirely on small fruits (manakins are major dispersers of tropical forest trees). Its habitat is tall, moist forest with an abundance of vines, and every nest that has been found so far has been in vegetation overhanging streams. The birds breed during the rains, and when the times of these vary, so does the breeding season. Presumably, in common with other manakins, the female performs all nesting and incubation duties, although for much of the year the species is seen in pairs.

Whatever we now know about it, the Araripe Manakin's future is still precarious, and the species is currently listed as Critically Endangered. Just to give an idea of its vulnerability: in 2005 an area where the manakins occur was ravaged by a large forest fire. Seven known nests were threatened, and it was only heroic action by the manakin research team (that included Weber Silva) in tackling the flames that prevented the nests from being destroyed altogether. This incident, in which the workers put their own lives at risk, shows how just a single disastrous event could almost destroy the population of a bird like the Araripe Manakin.

There is, however, a good deal of support for this striking species. Aside from the grants received to study it, the Araripe Manakin has also attracted financial help and very public accolades from the

Below: An illustration by Norman Arlott of the 'sweet-voiced bird of the bush', as the Noisy Scrub-bird is known on its 'memorial'.

MADAGASCAR POCHARD
Aythya innotata

was compromised again with the introduction of a couple of exotic plants, Water Hyacinth (*Eichhornia crassipes*) and Water-fern (*Salvinia* sp.), which replaced the lake's natural covering of waterlilies (*Nymphaea* spp.) and led to congestion and the deoxygenating of the water. In addition to all these changes, local people would occasionally trap waterbirds, including the pochard, using bait.

It is quite possible that the Madagascar Pochard could have survived all this, but the next blow came in the 1950s, when *Tilapia* fish were introduced to Lake Alaotra. This was especially destructive, because these fish are herbivores and reduced the rich stands of emergent vegetation on which the pochard depended. However, they were not the last sub-surface threat to invade the ducks' home. North American Black Bass (*Micropterus salmoides*) was introduced in the 1960s and may well have taken to predating young pochards. With so many changes bringing almost unbearable pressure on this duck in seemingly its last refuge on earth, it is hardly surprising that it could not last.

The truth is that, even today, Lake Alaotra is not really suitable for the Madagascar Pochard. Only a few of the above problems have been resolved or reduced, although happily there has been a comeback of waterlily-dominated vegetation in the south of the lake. But the whole ecosystem is still under threat. Madagascar is a desperately poor country, and Lake Alaotra is sorely needed for agriculture and fishing.

It was always likely to be another locality that saved the Madagascar Pochard, and in November 2006 two men researching the rare Madagascar Harrier (*Circus macrosceles*) stumbled upon the bird's secret hideaway. Biologists Dr Lily-Arison René de Roland and Thé Seing Sam, working for the Peregrine Fund, came upon a small volcanic lake called Bemanevika Lake, no less than 330km from Lake Alaotra. To their astonishment they found a flock of nine adults and four young, the highest number seen anywhere for 46 years. It was a particularly unexpected find because of what had been assumed about the pochard's biology. This lake was small and almost without any emergent vegetation, yet previously the birds had been assumed to be heavily dependent on a generous growth of waterlilies and other plants. The birds here were confounding expectations, in every sense.

They have continued to do so and, in view of the species's former desperate state, are almost thriving by comparison. Later visits by the Peregrine Fund Madagascar Project Team in 2006 revealed about 20 adults in all, with nine ducklings, and in 2008 there were 25 individuals and fully six pairs nesting on the lake. Further encouragement in 2006 came from an observation of five individuals at a second locality very close by, although those that saw the birds could not be sure that they were different from the original flock. If they were different, a higher population at two localities would boost survival prospects further.

For now, though, let's be grateful that they are on at least one lake, and that the site happens to be unsuitable for rice production and has no fish for people to catch. It seems that, especially with guards permanently stationed on-site to keep hunters out, the birds are probably safe for the moment. Meanwhile, the search goes on for any other remote hideaways in the same area where there could be more birds.

It is a remarkable turnaround for a species that had been all but written off. '*Innotata*' – not at all.

Left: White eyes identify this bird as a male Madagascar Pochard.

Below: These two precious ducklings would currently constitute a significant proportion (about 7 per cent) of the world population.

NIGHT PARROT
Pezoporus occidentalis

several haystacks. Furthermore, the bird itself is hardly co-operative. It is nocturnal, one of only two parrots in the world to be active only in darkness (the other is the Kakapo, see pages 20-23). It is also, despite being able to fly, largely ground-living, which means that it keeps itself hidden among the vegetation. Indeed, some early observers compared its secretive habits to that of a quail. Thirdly, it probably lives the typical outback nomadic lifestyle, following food supplies as they become available in different areas, making it mobile and even harder to pin down.

The difficulties have been exacerbated, if anything, by a long series of unconfirmed sight records that have given the bird more mystique by the year and made its status even more difficult to determine. For example, in 1979, scientists from the South Australian Museum observed a flock of four at Lake Perigundi, in the far north-west of their state. Furthermore, in 2005 two ecologists made quite prolonged observations of a couple of birds at a waterhole in the Pilbara region of Western Australia. Other claimed observations have been similarly far-flung, yet also similarly compelling. The descriptions are good, the observers reliable, the circumstances reasonable. All came from the Night Parrot's two known habitats in the arid zone, samphire (*Chenopodium*) shrubland and spinifex (*Triodium*) thickets. Yet with such a rare and iconic bird, with the stakes so high, sight records can never be taken as definitive proof of a bird's existence. The current painful search for Ivory-billed Woodpeckers (*Campephilus principalis*) in the USA would seem to bear this out, in which a blank has so far been drawn in following up truly believable sight records by

excellent observers (see pages 230-233). There is one difference, of course; there is definitive proof that the Night Parrot is still alive and well.

Furthermore, the record from Diamantina National Park suddenly raises the prospect that the Night Parrot's long game of hide and seek is about to come to an end. That is because the two recent records of roadside corpses were both within 200km of each other: Boulia, the nearest town to the location of the 1990 record, is north-west of Diamantina, in an area known as the Channel Country. Furthermore, there have also been recent sight records near Cloncurry, another 200km to the north. Is there now such a thing as the Night Parrot Triangle?

As yet we don't know. Despite the fact that the 2006 record caused a sensation when it was made public (there were many rumours at the time that it had been suppressed to prevent a scrum of bird tourism to the area), the Channel Country has since suffered from flooding, making the whole area hard to reach for a follow-up survey. At the time of writing, no more dead birds have come to light and, as yet, there have been no photographs or videos of live Night Parrots.

The intriguing nature of the Night Parrot's elusiveness was recently summed up well by one of Australia's leading conservationists. 'It could be critically endangered,' he commented (it is classified as such by BirdLife International), 'but equally, it could even be quite common. We simply don't know.'

And so the mystery remains.

Opposite: There's plenty of room in the outback for a small, ground-living, nocturnal parrot to hide. These are definitely not its tracks!

PINK-HEADED DUCK

Rhodonessa caryophyllacea

An extinct bird in the pink?

There are a whole suite of species that could find their way into the 'pending' section of this book. Extinction, by definition, is hard to prove, and even when a species has been missing for many years there will always be some hope that it survives. A number of species seem especially hard to consign to the extinct tray, as unconfirmed observations trickle out determinedly over the years, briefly raising expectancy before years of silence bring doubts once again. The Eskimo Curlew (*Numenius borealis*), last seen with certainty in 1981, is a good example: doubtful records still crop up regularly.

Of all the species that are in this category, though, there are one or two that really do seem to have better credentials for continued survival than the rest, and offer a genuine hope that they turn up again one day, even after many years of absence. And as author of this book, I have a hunch about one in particular, the Pink-headed Duck.

It might be reckoned as a long shot. After all, the last confirmed wild record was a long time ago, in 1949 in India, and the spate of rumours that inevitably accompany lost birds began to fade in the 1960s. The last specimen was collected in 1935, and the last of a number of ill-fated captive birds died in 1945 without ever successfully breeding. Surely, if the Pink-headed Duck isn't definitely extinct, what is?

This species is, or was, certainly a distinctive bird. It was large for a duck, as big as a Mallard (*Anas platyrhynchos*), and it had a long neck that was apparently held somewhat stiffly upright when the bird was swimming. The bill was big and very long, and pink. The male's body plumage was largely chocolate brown but, contrasting with this, the head and neck were a bizarrely garish pink, a highly unusual colour for any bird, let alone a duck. Although the female was less distinctive, with a faded version of the male's plumage, one could argue that it would be hard to mistake the Pink-headed Duck for anything else.

However, set against the unlikelihood of overlooking a large and uniquely patterned duck for six decades, there are a couple of good reasons to

Below: The Pink-headed Duck's distinctive appearance should make it easy to identify given a good view – but recent sight records have been brief and inconclusive.

WHITE-EYED RIVER MARTIN

Pseudochelidon sirintarae

The enigma in the reedbeds

This is the story of a bird that mysteriously appeared and disappeared, all in the course of a few years. Where it came from no-one knows, and its current whereabouts are equally a mystery. It remains one of the greatest enigmas of Asian ornithology.

On the evening of 28 January 1968, a strange bird found its way into a trap at Bung Boraphet, a large (25,000ha) lake in central Thailand. It was immediately obvious that it was something special. Bird ringers in the area, led by zoologist Kitti Thonglongya, marvelled in astonishment at the little alien's large, swollen white eyes, strong feet, narrow tail-streamers and velvety plumage. Although it was clearly in the swallow and martin family, they knew straight away that nothing of its kind had ever been described to science before. On the following night another of the strange martins was caught, and a little later, on 10 February, seven more. Some of these latter birds looked different to the first specimen, browner and with no tail streamers, and were assumed to be juveniles. But every one of them was so distinctive that there was never any question of their identity as the new species.

The White-eyed River Martin was formally described by Thonglongya shortly afterwards, and named in honour of Princess Sirindhorn Thepratanasuda, a member of the Thai royal family who is currently third in line to the throne. With its royal connection, unique appearance and scientific importance, the martin soon became a local celebrity, and a source of pride and curiosity to the Thai people.

It would be hard to overemphasize what a surprising discovery this was. Even in 1968, Thailand was already very well known ornithologically, with distinguished studies going back well over a hundred years. Furthermore, Bung Boraphet didn't exactly fit the profile as a type-locality for anything. It was a man-made lake and marsh created only in 1927 by the damming of the Nan River, with quite a large human population around it. It was, and still is, an important place for birds, but not quite the virgin territory that might be expected to harbour something unknown. It

Above: The White-eyed River Martin looks like no other hirundine, with its white eyes and long central tail-streamers.

has even been drained periodically, with all the ecological turbulence that this entails.

Whatever the conundrum of its appearance, the White-eyed River Martin was soon to deepen its mystery further, for its disappearance was almost as sudden as its appearance. Another specimen was obtained in the winter following the species' discovery at Bung Boraphet, and this is the bird in the photographs on these pages. A pair also found its way to a zoo in Bangkok in 1971. Interestingly, there is strong evidence that many others, perhaps up to 120, were caught by locals during the flurry of interest in the early 1970s and taken to nearby zoos or presented to dignitaries, but by the middle of that decade the trail of the White-eyed River Martin began to go cold. Apart from a record of six individuals flying over the lake on 3 February 1978, the rest is conjecture. Four were said to have been seen perched on trees on one

of the lake's islands in 1980, and there is a rumour of one trapped in 1986. However, since then, nothing. There haven't even been doubtful sight records, as there have for so many 'lost' species all over the world. Now, despite periodic thorough searches at Bung Boraphet and elsewhere, more than 20 years have passed without the merest trace of the bird, which is most unusual for such an iconic species.

There is one further point that makes the story intriguing, too. Although the White-eyed River Martin is generally thought to have been discovered by the ringing team, this is now known not to be the case. Bung Boraphet was used by local hunters, and the netting of the Barn Swallow roost where the martin had appeared, which probably then numbered in

227

New Holland Concise Bird Guide

Ideal field guide to British birds for adults or children. Covers more than 250 species in colour. Comes in durable plastic wallet and includes fold-out insert comparing species in flight. Also available in the series: *Butterflies & Moths* and *Wild Flowers*.
£4.99 ISBN 978 1 84773 601 7

New Holland European Bird Guide

Peter H Barthel. The only truly pocket-sized comprehensive field guide to all the birds of Britain and Europe. Features more than 1,700 beautiful and accurate artworks of more than 500 species.
£10.99 ISBN 978 1 84773 110 4

SASOL Birds of Southern Africa

Ian Sinclair, Phil Hockey and Warwick Tarboton. The world's leading guide to southern Africa's 950 bird species. Each is illustrated in full colour and has its own distribution map.
£19.99 ISBN 978 1 86872 721 6

The Slater Field Guide to Australian Birds

Peter Slater, Pat Slater and Raoul Slater. Fully updated edition of the comprehensive field guide. Features more than 750 species and 150 plates.
£14.99 ISBN 978 1 87706 963 5

Tales of a Tabloid Twitcher

Stuart Winter. The key birding events and personalities, scandal and gossip of the past two decades and beyond seen through the eyes of a the only British journalist who is a birdwatching fanatic. A 'must-read' book for all birders.
£7.99 ISBN 978 1 84773 693 2

Top 100 Birding Sites of the World

Dominic Couzens. An inspiration for the traveling birder. Brings together a selection of the best places to go birdwatching on Earth, covering every continent. Includes 350 photos and more than 100 maps.
£35.00 ISBN 978 1 84773 109 8

see www.newhollandpublishers.com for details and offers

Image credits

Photographs by (a = above, b = below, l = left, r = right): AGAMI (pages 5, 17, 24, 31l, 36, 43, 44, 49b, 50 [both], 53a, 57, 62, 63, 67, 69, 71b, 74, 75, 80, 83, 91r, 92, 93, 94, 97, 98, 100, 101, 105b, 108, 111 [both], 112, 113, 117b, 120, 123b, 124, 131, 133l, 135, 140, 141, 149, 153, 155, 158, 159, 168, 171l, 173a, 179 [both], 189 [both], 207, 217 and 225), Nick Athanas (page 53b), Paul Baker, U.S. Geological Survey (pages 143 and 145), Ashley Banwell (pages 198, 199 and 205), Arnoud van den Berg (pages 171r and 173b), BirdLife International Albatross Task Force (page 13b), Graeme S Chapman (page 193), Chaiwat Chinuparawat (pages 87, 89, 105l, 127), Bill Coster (pages 2, 14, 27, 29 and 154), Gerald Cubitt (pages 20, 23, 31r and 45), Martin Flade (page 85), David Geale (pages 139a, 212, 215 [both] and 216), Phil Gregory (pages 47 [both], 48 and 49a), Louis A Hansen/The Natural History and Zoological Museums, University of Copenhagen (pages 183, 184 and 185), Greg Homel (page 156), Dieter Hoppe/BirdLife International (page 167a), Jon Hornbuckle (page 65), Rob Hutchinson (page 197), Hannu Jännes (pages 33, 34 and 35), Jack Jeffrey (page 144), M Kelsey/BirdLife International (page 165b), Kanit Khanikul (pages 8, 161 and 163 [both]), Tim Laman (pages 40 [both] and 41), Tomer Landsberger (page 110), Luis Claudio Marigo/BirdLife International (page 165a), H E McClure/BirdLife International (pages 227, 228 (both) and 229), Gerald McCormack/BirdLife International (page 13a), Ian Merrill (pages 73, 133r and 137b), Pete Morris (pages 3, 39, 115, 119, 137a, 139b, 180, 186, 187, 209, 211 [both]), Phil Palmer (pages 1, 61, 91l, 129b), Simon Papps (pages 19 [both], 55, 56, 88, 129a and 151l), Ed Parnell/BirdLife International (page 221), ProAves Colombia (page 78), Paddy Ryan (front cover and page 21), Roger Safford (pages 175 and 177), Bill Schmoker (page 151l), Brent Stephenson (pages 190, 201a and 203), James T. Tanner (pages 11, 231r, 232 and 233 [both]), Bryan Thomas (pages 201b and 202), Jørgen Thompsen/BirdLife International (page 167b), David Tipling (pages 16, 26, 36, 102, 107, 117l, 121, 123a, 134), Nigel Voaden (pages 58, 77 and 79) and Mike Weedon (pages 70 and 71a).

Artwork by Norman Arlott/BirdLife International (pages 195, 219 and 223) and Peter Hayman/BirdLife International (page 231l).

INDEX

Pagination in **bold** refers to featured birds.